# One-Handed Basket Weaving

# RUMI

## *One-Handed Basket Weaving*

### POEMS ON
### THE THEME OF WORK

VERSIONS BY
## Coleman Barks

MAYPOP   Athens, Georgia

# M A Y P O P

Grateful acknowledgment is made to Random House
for permission to reprint from Studs Terkel's *Working*.

*Cover:* Water coming over the old Puritan Cord millpond dam
between Athens and Watkinsville, Georgia. Photo by Benjamin
Barks. The cane-threaded script was Cole Barks' idea.

**RUMI: One-Handed Basket Weaving**
  $9.00/copy, plus $1.50 postage and handling,
  50¢ postage for each additional book.

*Order from:*

MAYPOP
196 Westview Drive
Athens, GA 30606

(404) 543-2148

ISBN 0-9618916-3-7
Library of Congress Catalog Card Number 91-62710

*For those who come to the "birdcage,"
the upstairs, screened-in porch,
and for the piece of work itself.*

# Contents

## Rumi's Life

Persians and Afghanis call Rumi "Jalaluddin Balkhi." His family lived in Balkh (Afghanistan), or rather, as we know from recent scholarship, in the nearby town of Waksh. The name "Rumi" means "from Roman Anatolia." He was not known by that name, of course, until after his family, fleeing the threat of the invading Mongol armies, emigrated to Konya (Turkey), sometime between 1215 and 1220. Rumi was born September 30, 1207.

His father, Bahauddin Walad, was a theologian and jurist, and a mystic of uncertain lineage. His *Maarif*, a collection of notes, diary-like remarks, sermons, and strange accounts of visionary experiences, has shocked most of the conventional scholars who have tried to understand them. He shows a startlingly sensual freedom (I am told) in saying his union with God.

"Go into God, and He will take you into Him, and kiss you and show Himself to you, so that you may not run away. Your whole heart will stay there day and night."

*(Maarif,* 28)[1]

Rumi was instructed in his father's secret inner life by a former student of his father, Burhanuddin Mahaqqiq. Burhan and Rumi also studied Sanai and Attar. It was Sanai who composed the first *mathnawi,* the mystical teaching form that Rumi was later to perfect. At his father's death Rumi took over the position of sheikh in the dervish learning community in Konya. His life seems to have been a fairly normal one for a religious scholar — teaching, meditating, helping the poor — until in late October of 1244 when he met a stranger on the road who put a question to him. We cannot be entirely certain of the question, but it made the

[1] Quoted in Annemarie Schimmel's manuscript to be published in 1992 by Shambhala Press, *I Am Wind, You are Fire: The Life and Works of Jalaloddin Rumi.* As far as I know, the *Maarif* of Rumi's father has not been translated into English, except for small excerpts in Professor Schimmel's work. Many other references in this account of Rumi's life also rely on her indispensable scholarship.

learned professor faint to the ground. It was spoken by the wandering dervish, Shams of Tabriz, and according to the most reliable account he asked who was greater, Muhammed or Bestami, for Bestami had said, "How great is my glory," whereas Muhammed had acknowledged in his prayer to God, "We do not know You as we should."

Rumi was finally able to answer that Muhammed was greater, because Bestami had taken one gulp of the divine and stopped there, whereas for Muhammed the way was always unfolding. There are various versions of this encounter, but whatever the "facts," the two became inseparable. Their Friendship is one of the mysteries. They were together for months without any human needs, translated into a region of pure conversation. This ecstatic connection caused difficulties in the religious community. Rumi's students felt neglected. Sensing the trouble, Shams disappeared as suddenly as he had appeared. Annemarie Schimmel thinks that it was at this first disappearance that Rumi began the transformation into a mystical artist. "He turned into a poet, began to listen to music, and sang, whirling around, hour after hour."

Word came that Shams was in Damascus. Rumi sent his son, Sultan Walad, to Syria to bring his Friend back to Konya. When Rumi and Shams met for the second time, they fell at each other's feet, so that "no one knew who was lover and who the Beloved." Shams stayed in Rumi's home and was married to a young girl who had been brought up in the family. Again the long mystical conversation (sohbet) began, and again the jealousies grew.

On the night of December 5, 1248, as Rumi and Shams were talking, Shams was called from the back door. He went out, never to be seen again. Most likely, he was murdered with the connivance of Rumi's son, Allaedin, but the mystery of the Friend's absence covered Rumi's world. He himself went out searching for Shams. He journeyed again to Damascus, and it was there that he realized,

> "Why should I seek? I am the same
> as he. His essence speaks through me.
> I have been looking for myself!"

The union became complete. There was full *fana,* annihilation in the Friend. Shams was writing the poems. The collection of Rumi's odes and quatrains is still called *The Works of Shams of Tabriz.* Who is this Shams? It's difficult to know. Before he met Rumi, he had traveled throughout the Near East searching and praying for someone who could "endure my company."

After Shams' death, and Rumi's merging with him, another companion was found, Saladin Zarkub, the goldsmith. The story has often been told of how Rumi was walking through the goldsmithing bazaar in Konya, and the sound of their hammering started him whirling in ecstasy. He took Saladin by the hand and led him dancing into the street. Saladin then became the Friend that Rumi addressed his poems to, not so fierily as to Shams, but with a quiet tenderness. When Saladin died, Husam Chelebi, Rumi's scribe and favorite student, assumed this role. Rumi claimed that Husam was the source and the one who understood the vast, secret order of the *Mathnawi,*[1] which shifts so amazingly from theory to folklore to jokes to ecstatic poetry. For the last twelve years of his life Rumi dictated the six volumes of this masterwork to Husam. He died on December 17, 1273.

---

[1] All poetry here comes from this work. I have used as a source Reynold Nicholson's translation, *The Mathnawi of Jalaluddin Rumi* (8 vols., London: Luzac & Co., 1925–40).

## One-Handed Basket Weaving

There was a dervish who lived alone in the mountains,
who made a vow never to pick fruit from the trees,
or to shake them down,
or to ask anyone to pick fruit for him.

"Only what the wind makes fall."
This was his way
of giving in to God's will.

There is a traditional saying from the Prophet
that a human being is like a feather in the desert
being blown about wherever the wind takes it.

So for a while in the joy of this surrender
he woke each dawn with a new direction to follow.

But then came five days with no wind,
and no pears fell.

He patiently restrained himself,
until a breeze blew just strong enough
to lower a bough full of ripe pears
close to his hand, but not strong enough
to detach the pears.

He reached out and picked one.

Nearby, a band of thieves were dividing
what they had stolen.

The authorities surprised them and immediately
began the punishments: the severing
of right hands and left feet.

The hermit was seized by mistake
and his hand cut off,
but before his foot could be severed also,
he was recognized.

The prefect came. "Forgive these men.
They did not know. Forgive us all!"

The sheikh said, "This is not your fault.
I broke my vow, and the Beloved
has punished me."

He became known as Sheikh Aqta,
which means, "The teacher
whose hand has been cut off."

One day a visitor entered his hut without knocking
and saw him weaving palm leaf baskets.
It takes two hands to weave!

"Why have you entered without warning?"

"Out of love for you."

"Then keep this secret which you see
has been given to me."

But others began to know about this,
and many came to the hut to watch.

The hand that helped
when he was weaving palm leaves
came because he no longer had any fear
of dismemberment or death.

When those anxious, self-protecting
imaginations leave, the real,
cooperative work begins.

(III, 1634-1642, 1672-1690, 1704-1720)

## Awkward Comparison

This physical world has no two things alike.
Every comparison is awkwardly rough.

You can put a lion next to a man,
but the placing is hazardous to both.

Say the body is like this lamp.
It has to have a wick and oil. Sleep and food.
If it doesn't get those, it will die,
and it's always burning those up, trying to die.

But where is the sun in this comparison?
It rises, and the lamp's light
mixes with the day.
                    Oneness,
which is the reality, cannot be understood
with lamp and sun images. The blurring
of a plural into a unity is wrong.

No image can describe
what of our fathers and mothers,
our grandfathers and grandmothers, remains.

Language does not touch the One
who lives in each of us.

**(IV, 419-433)**

## Snow and the Voice

After Bestami died, it happened
as he said it would, that Bu'l-Hasan
became the sheikh for the community,
and every day he would go to Bestami's tomb
to receive instruction.

Bu'l-Hasan had been told to do this
in a dream, by Bestami himself.

Every dawn he went and stood facing the grave
until mid-morning. Either the spirit of Bestami
would come and talk to him, or in silence
the questions he had would be answered.

But one day a deep snow had fallen.
The graves were piled together
and indistinguishable.

Bu'l-Hasan felt lost.
Then he heard the sheikh's voice.

"The world is made of snow. It falls and melts
and falls again. Don't be concerned
with that. Come toward the sound
of my voice. Always move
in this direction."
                    And from that day
Bu'l-Hasan began to experience
the enlightened state
which he had only heard
and read about
before.

                                        (IV, 1925-1934)

## Love for Certain Work

Traveling is as refreshing for some
as staying at home is for others.

Solitude in a mountain place
fills with companionship
for this one,
                and dead-weariness
for that one.
                This person loves
being in charge of the workings
of a community.
                This one loves
the ways that heated iron can be shaped
with a hammer.
                Each has been given
a strong desire for certain work.

A *love* for those motions,
and all motion is love.

The way sticks and pieces of dead grass and leaves
shift about in the wind
and with the directions of rain and puddle-water
on the ground, those motions
are all a following
of the love they've been given.

                                        (III, 1616-1619)

## The Hoopoe's Talent

Whenever a pavilion was pitched in the countryside
for Solomon, the birds would come
to pay their respects and talk with him.

Solomon understood bird-language.
There was no confused twittering
in his presence. Each species spoke
its call distinctly.

Being understood is such a joy!
When a person is with people
that he or she cannot confide in,
it's like being tied up.

And I don't mean a cultural kinship.
There are Indians and Turks who speak the same language.
There are Turks who don't understand each other.

I'm talking of those who are inside
the one love together.
                    So, the birds were asking Solomon
questions and telling him their special talents.
They all hoped that they would be asked
to stay in Solomon's presence.
It came the turn of the hoopoe.
                              "My king,
I have only one talent, but I hope
it will be helpful to you."
                    "Say it."
"When I fly to the highest point
of my ability and look down,
I can see then through the earth
to the water table.

I can see whether it's muddy with clay,
or clear, running through stone.

I can see where the springs are,
and where good wells may be dug."

Solomon replied, "You will make a fine companion
for my expeditions into the wilderness!"

The jealous crow couldn't stand it.
He yelled out,
              "If hoopoe has such keen eyesight,
why did she not see the snare
that caught her once?"
                    "Good question," said Solomon.
"What about this, hoopoe?"
                    "My water-seeing talent
is a true one. And it's also true
that I have been blind to things
that have trapped me. There is a will
beyond my knowing that causes
both my blindness and my clairvoyance.
Crow doesn't acknowledge that."

                              (I, 1202-1233)

## Looking into the Creek

The way the soul is
with the senses and the intellect
is like a creek.

When desire-weeds grow thick,
the intelligence can't flow,
and soul-creatures stay hidden.

But sometimes your reasonable mind
runs so strong it clears
the clogged stream
as though with God's hand.

No longer weeping and frustrated,
your being grows as powerful
as your wantings were before.

Laughing and satisfied, that masterful flowing
lets soul-creatures appear.

You look down,
and it's lucid dreaming.

The gates made of light
swing open. You see in.

(III, 1824-1834)

## A Just Finishing Candle

A candle is made to become entirely flame.
In that annihilating moment
it has no shadow.

It is nothing but a tongue of light
describing a refuge.

Look at this
just-finishing candle stub
as someone who is finally safe
from virtue and vice,

the pride and the shame
we claim from those.

(V, 672-682)

## This We Have Now

This we have now
is not imagination.

This is not
grief or joy.

Not a judging state,
or an elation,
or sadness.

Those come
and go.

This is the presence
that doesn't.

It's dawn, Husam,
here in the splendor of coral,
inside the Friend, the simple truth
of what Hallaj said.

What else could human beings want?

When grapes turn to wine,
they're wanting
this.

When the nightsky pours by,
it's really a crowd of beggars,
and they all want some of this!

This
that we are now
created the body, cell by cell,
like bees building a honeycomb.

The human body and the universe
grew from this, not this
from the universe and the human body.

(I, 1803-1813)

## The Man with a Bear

For the man who saved the bear
from the dragon's mouth, the bear
became a sort of a pet.

When he would lie down to rest,
the bear would stand guard.

A certain friend passed by.
"Brother, how did this bear
get connected to you?"

He told the adventure with the dragon,
and the friend responded,
                    "Don't forget
what your companion is. This friend
is *not* human! It would be better
to choose one of your own kind."

"You're just jealous of my unusual helper.
Look at his sweet devotion. Ignore
the bearishness!"

But the friend was not convinced.
"Don't go into the forest
with a comrade like this!
Let me go with you."
                    "I'm tired.
Leave me alone."
                    The man began imagining
motives other than kindness for his friend's concern.
"He has made a bet with someone
that he can separate me from my bear." Or,
"He will attack me when my bear is gone."

He had begun to think like a bear!

So the human friends went different ways,
the one with his bear into a forest,
where he fell asleep again.

The bear stood over him
waving the flies away.

But the flies kept coming back,
which irritated the bear.

He dislodged a stone from the mountainside
and raised it over the sleeping man.

When he saw that the flies had returned
and settled comfortably on the man's face,
he slammed the stone down, crushing
to powder the man's face and skull.

Which proves the old saying:

IF YOU'RE FRIENDS
WITH A BEAR,
THE FRIENDSHIP
WILL DESTROY YOU.

WITH THAT ONE,
IT'S BETTER TO BE
ENEMIES.

(II, 2010-2035, 2125-2130)

## Night-Thieves

There was a king roaming his country at night.
He met up with a band of thieves.
                              "Who are you?"
they asked.
            "I am one of you."
                              So they walked together,
and each of them spoke of the special skill
that suited him for this night-work.
                              One said,
"My genius is in my ears. I can understand
what a dog is saying when it barks."
                              The others laughed,
"Not much value in that!"
                       Another thief said,
"My specialty is in my eyes.
                       Whatever I see by night,
I can recognize also in daylight."
                       Another, "My strength
is in my arm. I can tunnel through any wall!"
                                   Another,
"My nose. I can sniff the ground and know
where treasure's hidden."
                   And the last thief revealed,
"It's my hand. I can throw a lasso
around anything."

Then they asked the king-in-disguise
what his contribution was.
                     "It's this beard.
Whenever I turn it toward criminals,
they are freed!"
                "Oho! You *are* a good one
to have with us!"
                   And they continued on, as it happened,
toward the palace.
                A watchdog barked,
and the listener-thief interpreted,
                         "He's saying,

25

'The king is with us!'"
                    The sniffer-thief smelt
the ground. "This is prime land."
                         The lassoer
quickly threw a rope over the wall.
                              The tunneler
tunneled into the treasury, and they all
loaded up with gold embroidery and huge pearls.

The king watched,
and then slipped quietly away.

The next day the robbery was discovered,
and the king sent his guards
to make the arrests.

As the thieves were brought in,
the one who could recognize night things by day
said,
     "This is the friend
who went with us last night,
the beard man!"

This night & day man was a mystic.
He understood what had happened.
                         "This king
embodies the text that says,
               *and He is with you.*
He knows our secrets.
He played our game with us.

This king is the Witness,
and in his clear truthfulness
is the grace we most deeply need."

                    (VI, 2816-2825, 2833-2859, 2867-2870)

*The City of Saba*

Once in the city of Saba
there was a glut of wealth.

Everyone had *more* than enough.
Even the bath-stokers wore gold belts.

Huge grape clusters hung down
on every street and brushed the faces
of the citizens. No one had to do
*anything.*
         You could balance
an empty basket on your head and walk
through any orchard, and it would fill
by itself with overripe fruit
dropping into it.
             Stray dogs strayed
in lanes full of thrown-out scraps
with barely a notice.
                The lean desert wolf
got indigestion from the rich food.

Everyone was fat and satiated
with all the extra.
              There were no robbers.
There was no energy for crime,
or for gratitude.
             And no one wondered
about the unseen world. The people of Saba
felt bored with just the *mention* of prophecy.

They had no desire of any kind. Maybe
some idle curiosity about miracles,
but that was it.
            This over-richness
is a subtle disease. Those who have it
are blind to what's wrong, and deaf
to anyone who points it out.
                    The city of Saba
can not be understood from within itself!

27

But there is a cure,
an individual medicine,
not a social remedy:
                    Sit quietly, and listen
for a voice within that will say,
                        *Be more silent.*
As that happens,
                    your soul starts to revive.
Give up talking, and your positions of power.
Give up the excessive money.
                        Turn toward the teachers
and the prophets who don't live in Saba.

They can help you grow sweet again
and fragrant and wild and fresh
and thankful for any small event.

                    (III, 2656-2667, 2675-2680, 2726-2732)

## Story-Water

A story is like the water
you heat for your bath.

It takes messages between the fire
and your skin. It lets them meet,
and it cleans you!

Very few can sit down
in the middle of the fire itself
like a salamander or Abraham.
We need intermediaries.

A feeling of fullness comes,
but usually it takes some bread
to bring it.

Beauty surrounds us,
but usually we need to be walking
in a garden to know it.

The body itself is a screen
to shield and partially reveal
the light that's blazing
inside your presence.

Water, stories, the body,
all the things we do, are mediums
that hide and show what's hidden.

Study them,
and enjoy this being washed
with a secret we sometimes know,
and then not.

(V, 228-236)

*One Song*

What is praised is One,
so the praise is One, too,
many jugs being emptied
into a huge basin.

All religions,
all this singing,
is one song.

The differences are just
illusion and vanity.

The sun's light looks a little different
on this wall than it does on that wall,
and a lot different on this other one,
but it's still one light.

We have borrowed these clothes,
these time and place personalities,
from a light, and when we praise,
we're pouring them back in.

(III, 2122-2127)

## Mary's Hiding

Before these possessions you love
slip away, say
            what Mary said
when she was surprised by Gabriel,

    "I'll hide inside God."

Naked in her room
she saw a form of beauty
that could give her new life.

Like the sun coming up,
or a rose as it opens.

And she leaped, as her habit was,
out of herself
            into the divine presence.

There was fire in the channel of her breath.
The light and the majesty came.

I am smoke from that fire,
and proof of its existence,
more than any external form.

                              (III, 3700-3720)

## Lead On, Husam

Husam, I feel your pull again,
drawing this *Mathnawi* God knows where!

Through you, this book is no longer
made of reflected light. We've gone beyond
the moon, and now you want to add more!

God must want it, if you want it.
I used to say of you, "He belongs to God,"
but now, "God belongs to him,"
comes as the answer.

Thousands of times the words of this book
are saying *Thank you, Husam.*
*Thank you, Husam!*
                    Such gratitude always brings
more happiness, just as nearness to God
comes with genuine humility.

This book doesn't grow longer to be applauded.
It grows like a vineyard in summer.

I've called you *Radiance,*
and a *Sword of Light.*

Your presence is the sun, a bright blade
with more dignity and clarity than moonlight.

People lose the road in that pale fog.
Then the sun comes up, and they find the way.

Markets never stay open
with just the moon to light them,
because it's impossible then
to tell good coins from bad.

So lead on, Husam,
my patient and joyful commander.

It's dawn, and this caravan
is starting out again!

(IV, 1-24)

## The Dream That Must Be Interpreted

This place is a dream.
Only a sleeper considers it real.

Then death comes like dawn,
and you wake up laughing
at what you thought was your grief.

But there's a difference with *this* dream.
Everything cruel and unconscious
done in the illusion of the present world,
all that does not fade away at the death-waking.

It stays,
and it must be *interpreted*.

All the mean laughing,
all the quick, sexual wanting,
those torn coats of Joseph,
they change into powerful wolves
that you must face.

The retaliation that sometimes comes now,
the swift, payback hit,
is just a boy's game
to what the other will be.

You know about circumcision here.
It's full castration there!

And this groggy time we live,
this is what it's like:
                    A man goes to sleep in the town
where he has always lived, and he dreams he's living
in another town.
                    In the dream, he doesn't remember
the town he's sleeping in his bed in. He believes
the reality of the dream-town.

The world is that kind of sleep.

The dust of many crumbled cities
settles over us like a forgetful doze,
but we are older than those cities.

                                     We began
as a mineral. We emerged into plant life
and into the animal state, and then into being human,
and always we have forgotten our former states,
except in early spring when we slightly recall
being green again.

                         That's how a young person turns
toward a teacher. That's how a baby leans
toward the breast, without knowing the secret
of its desire, yet turning instinctively.

Humankind is being led along an evolving course,
through this migration of intelligences,
and though we seem to be sleeping,
there is an inner wakefulness
that directs the dream,

and that will eventually startle us back
to the truth of who we are.

(IV, 3654-3667, 3628-3652)

## The King's Falcon

The king had a noble falcon,
who wandered away one day,
and into the tent of an old woman,
who was making dumpling stew
for her children.
                    "Who's been taking care
of you?" she asked, quickly tying
the falcon's foot.
                    She clipped
his magnificent wings and cut
his fierce talons and fed him straw.
                                        "Someone
who doesn't know how to treat falcons,"
she answered herself,
                        "but your mother knows!"
Friend, this kind of talk is a prison.
Don't listen!
                    The king spent all day
looking for his falcon, and came at last
to that tent and saw his fine raptor
standing on a shelf in the smoky steam
of the old woman's cooking.
                              "You left me
for this?"
                    The falcon rubbed his wings
against the king's hand, feeling wordlessly
what was almost lost.
                        This falcon is like one who,
through grace, gets to sit close to the king,
and so thinks he's on the same level
as the king.
                    Then he turns his head for a moment,
and he's in the old woman's tent.

Don't feel *special*
in the king's presence.
Be mannerly and thankful
and very humble.

A falcon is an image of that part of you
that belongs with the king.

Once, there was a blind falcon
who fell in with owls in a wilderness.
They thought he wanted to take over the ruin
they were living in. They tore at his feathers.
"Wait! I have no interest in this place.
My home is the forearm of the king."

The owls thought
this was some kind of bragging trick
to distract them.
                    "No! I don't claim to be *like*
the king. I am a ragged, blind falcon.
All I can do is listen for the king's drum
and fly toward the sound when I hear it.

I am not of the king's species or genus,
but I have taken in some of the king's light,
the way air is swept up into a fire,
the way water becomes plant.

My ego has died into the king's being.
I roll in the dust at the feet of his horse.

Don't let this
blind-falcon form
fool you.

I am really a delicious dessert
that you should taste now, you owls,
before I hear the drum again,
because then I'll be gone."

(II, 323-341, 1131-1146, 1156-1177)

## The Level of Words

God has said,
                "The images that come
with human language
do not correspond to me,
but those who love words
must use them to come near."

Just remember,
                it's like saying of the king,
"He is not a weaver."
                                Is that praise?
Whatever such a statement is,
words are on *that* level
of God-knowledge.

(II, 1716-1719)

## Work in the Invisible

The Prophets have wondered to themselves,
"How *long*
should we keep pounding this cold iron? How *long*
do we have to whisper into an empty cage?"

Every motion of created beings
comes from the creator.

The first soul pushes,
and your second soul responds.

So don't be timid.
Load the ship and set out.

No one knows for certain
whether the vessel will sink
or reach the harbor.

Just don't be one of those merchants
who won't risk the ocean!

This is much more important
than losing or making money!

This is your connection to God.

Think of the fear and the hope that you have
about your livelihood. They make you
go to work diligently every day.

Now consider what the prophets have done.
Abraham wore fire for an anklet.
Moses spoke to the sea.
David moulded iron.
Solomon rode the wind.

Work in the invisible world
at least as hard
as you do in the visible.

Be companions with the prophets
even though no one here will know that you are,
not even the helpers of the Qutb, the abdals.

You can't imagine what *profit* will come!
When one of those generous ones
invites you into his fire,
go quickly!
   Don't say,
"But will it burn me? Will it hurt?"

(III, 3077-3109)

*Resurrection Day*

On Resurrection Day
God will say,
          "What did you do
with the strength and the energy
that your food gave you
on Earth?

How did you use your eyes?
What did you make with your five senses
while they were dimming and playing out?

I gave you hands and feet as tools
for preparing the ground for planting.

Did you, in the health I gave,
do the plowing?"

You will not be able to stand
when you hear those questions.

You will bend double with shame,
and finally acknowledge the glory.

God will then say,
          "Lift your head,
and answer these questions."

Your head will rise a little
and then slump again.
                    "Look at me!
Tell me what you've done."

You try, but you fall back
flat as a snake.
                    "I want every detail!
Tell me!"
          Eventually you'll be able to get
to a sitting position.
                         "Be plain and clear.
I have given you such gifts. What did you
do with them?"

Then you will turn to the right
looking to the prophets for help, as though
to say,
> I am stuck in the mud of my life.
> Help me out of this!
                        And they will answer,
those kings,
            "The time for helping is past.
The plow stands there in the field.
You should have used it."

Then you will turn to the left,
where your family is,
and they will say,
                "Don't look at us!
This conversation is between you
and your creator!"
                        Then you will pray the prayer
that is the essence of every ritual: God,
I have no hope. I am torn to shreds.
You are my first and my last
and my only refuge.

Don't do daily prayers like a bird
pecking its head up and down.

Prayer is an egg.
Hatch out
the total helplessness
inside.

                                    (III, 2149-2175)

41

## The Treasure's Nearness

A man searching for spiritual treasure
could not find it, so he was praying.

A voice inside said, "You were given
the intuition to shoot an arrow,
and then dig where it landed,

but you shot with all your archery skill!
You were told to draw the bow
with only a *fraction* of your ability."

What you are looking for
is nearer than the big vein
on your neck! Let the arrow drop.

Don't exhaust yourself like the philosophers,
who strain to shoot the high arcs
of their thought-arrows.

The more skill you use, the farther you'll be
from what your deepest love wants.

(VI, 2347-2351)

## How It Is with Grapes

Under the aegis of Solomon
the deer and the leopard were friends.

The dove rode safely in the hawk's talons.
Sheep did not panic when a wolf came near.

Solomon is the intelligence
that connects former enemies.

Don't look for bits of grain like an ant.
Look for the granary master,
and you'll have grain and the Presence
as well. Solomon lives now!

God has said there will never be a time
without a Solomon. In that consciousness
there is no guile, and inside it
your soul-birds sing unanimously.

They don't argue. There were once two tribes
in the Ansar region, but, it's told,
when they felt Muhammed's light,
old grudges disappeared, and they combined.

You know the way it is
with grapes, and with human beings!

When we're immature, we jostle competitively
in the bunch. Then we mature and soften.
Our skins rip open, and we become one juice!

We grow in that way through
the breath of a heart-master.

Now, some grapes stay stone-hard,
but the secret of what causes that
sour tightness must remain hidden.

Most grapes mature.
Blessings on the love
that gathers dust-grains
into the mud of turning pots!

But that's a bad metaphor.
The unity of the soul
has no likeness.

Just remember, Solomon lives nearby!
Don't scout the horizon for his presence.

As a man sleeping in a house
is not aware of the house, in that same way
you are not conscious of Solomon,
even though he's your shelter.

Don't be addicted to subtle discussions,
tying and untying knots, posing difficulties
that then you resolve.

Doing that, you're like a bird
who learns how to loosen the snare
and then fastens it again,
to show off his strange, new skill.

Don't forget that the point is to escape!
Remember how it feels to sail the mountain air
and smell the sweetness of the high meadows.

(II, 3700-3736)

## How Intelligence Advises Your Spirit

In the realm of your consciousness
there are two kings, and two advisors.

Solomon and Asaf, Pharaoh and Haman.
Sometimes Moses tells your Pharoah
something of such tenderness that
it would make the rocks give milk,

and then your mean-spirited advisor,
Haman, whose nature it is to hate,
comments, "Do you listen now
to men dressed in rags!"

And the glass house of loving language
gets destroyed by a ballistic stone.

Your Solomon has a different advisor.
With those two it is *Light upon Light,*
two perfumes mixing.

The inner king is your spirit.
The inner advisor, your intelligence.

When that counselor bows to your sensuality,
the advice is poisonous, but when he looks further
than just getting what's wanted at the moment,
then you're connected with Solomon.

Don't think that these are just names!
They're realities. Explore them.

Every morning Solomon comes to the mosque
not built by hands and sees a new plant
growing there. He asks, "Are you a medicine?
What is your name and your usefulness?"

Each morning the new plant tells him
its nature. "I am helpful to this condition
and detrimental to that, and such is
my name on the unseen tablets."

Solomon relates the information
to his physicians, and they write it down,
so the body may be relieved of pain.

Knowledge of medicine, and of astronomy, comes
in this way from the universal intellect,
not from the particular mind.

All tools and crafts were given
by that wider intelligence
and then modified by the individual mind.

Learn from Solomon.
Be apprenticed to him.

Master the craft he teaches,
and then practice it.

(IV, 1240-1261,1285-1300)

## Questions About Devastation

A man was breaking up the soil,
when another man came by, *"Why
are you ruining this land?"*

"Don't be a fool! Nothing can grow
until the ground is turned over and crumbled.

There can be no roses and no orchard
without first this that looks devastating.

You must lance an ulcer to heal it.
You must tear down parts of an old building
to restore it, and so it is with a sensual life
that has no spirit in it.
                    To change,
a person must face the dragon of his appetites
with another dragon, the life-energy
of the soul."
                When that's not strong,
the world seems to be full of people
who have your own fears and wantings.

As one thinks the room is spinning
when he's whirling around.

When your love contracts in anger,
the atmosphere itself feels threatening.

But when you're expansive, no matter
what the weather, you're in an open,
windy field with friends.

Many people travel to Syria and Iraq
and meet only hypocrites.

Others go all the way to India
and see just merchants buying and selling.

Others go to Turkestan and China
and find those countries filled
with sneak-thieves and cheats.

We always see the qualities

that are living in us.

A cow may walk from one side of the amazing city
of Baghdad to the other and notice only
a watermelon rind and a tuft of hay
that fell off a wagon.

Don't keep repeatedly doing
what your animal-soul wants to do.

That's like deciding to be a strip of meat
nailed and drying on a board in the sun.

Your spirit needs to follow the changes happening
in the spacious place it knows about.

*There,* the scene is always new,
a clairvoyant river of picturing,
more beautiful than any on earth.

This is where the sufis wash.
Purify your eyes, and see the pure world.
Your life will fill with radiant forms.

It's a question of cleaning
and then developing the spiritual senses.

Say you were blindfolded,
and a lovely woman came by.

You could know her beauty somewhat
by hearing her speak, but what
if she didn't say anything!

Muinuddin, there are marvels
you're not aware of. Don't judge with *your* eyes.
Look at me through *my* eyes.

See beyond phenomena,
and these difficult questions will dissolve
into love within love.

Peace be with you, sir,
in your position of leadership.

(IV, 2341-2358,2366-2383)

## The "Here I Am" Answer

The kindness in your look
is married to the substance
of your eyes.

Joy lives in the kidneys.
Grief in the liver.

Intelligence, that bright candle,
is burning in the matter
of your brain.

These connections have a purpose,
but we don't know what it is.

The universal soul touches
an individual soul and gives it
a pearl to hide in the chest.

A new Christ lives in you
from that touch, but no one
can say why or how.

Every word I say
is trying to coax a response
from that.
          "Lord," I call out,
and inside my "Lord" comes,
                    "Here I am,"
a "Here I am"
          that can't be heard,
but it can be tasted and felt
in every cell of the body.

(II, 1180-1191)

## Out in the Open Air

There is a kind of food
not taken in through the mouth:

Bits of knowing that nourish love.
The body and the human personality form a cup.
Every time you meet someone, something is poured in.

When two planets draw near,
they affect each other.

A man and a woman come together,
and a new human being appears.

Iron and stone converge,
and there are sparks.

Rain soaks the ground,
and fruits get juicy.

Human beings walk into a ripe orchard,
and a happiness enters their souls.

From that joy
emerges generosity.

From being out in the open air,
appetites sharpen.

The blush on our faces
comes from the sun.

There is a majesty in these connections,
a grandeur that is an invisible quality.

The sun I mention is Shams.
I could not live without his light,
as a fish needs water, as a worker
must appear in his work, as every being
pastures on the meadow of the Absolute:

Muhammed's horse, Boraq, Arabian stallions,
and even donkeys, every creature grazes there,
whether they know it or not.

Husam, heal the madness of these
who feel jealous of the sun!
Put a salve on their eyes,
and let them see that what they are wanting
is the extinction of light!

(II, 1089-1128)

## The Way That Moves As You Move

Some commentary on the verse,
*As you start on the Way, the Way appears.*
*When you cease to be, Real Being comes.*

Zuleikha shut every door,
but Joseph kept rattling the locks.
He trusted, and kept moving back and forth,
and somehow he escaped.

This is the way you slip through
into your non-spatial home.

Think how you came into this world.
Can you explain how that was? No?
The same way you came, you'll leave.

You wander landscapes in your dreams.
How did you get there?

Close your eyes and surrender,
and find yourself in the city of God.

But you're still looking for admiration.
You love how your customers look at you.
You love to sit at the head of the assembly.

You close your eyes and see people applauding,
as surely as an owl shuts and sees the forest.

You live in an admiration-world,
but what do you offer your admirers?

If you had true spiritual gifts to give,
you wouldn't think of customers.

There was once a man who said, "I am a prophet.
In fact, I am the edge of prophecy
moving through time."

People surrounded him and tied him up
and brought him before the king.

"What right does this man have to say
that he lives in the place of revelation?"

The man himself spoke up, "Think how an infant sleeps
and grows *unconsciously* into awareness.

Prophets are not like that. They pass, waking,
from the source to this up-and-down
of the five senses, this left-right,
back-and-forth world."

"Put him on the rack," they screamed.
But the king saw that the man was thin
and fragile. He spoke gently. Kindness
was his way. He dispersed the crowd,
and sat the man down, and asked him
where he lived.
                "My home is the peace of God,
but I have come to this judging place,
where no one knows me. I feel like a fish
trying to live on sand."
                        The king kept trying
to joke him out of this state. "But why
did you make these claims *today*? Was it
something you ate?"
                "I don't care about world-food.
I am tasting the God's honey, but what is that
to these people? They're like mountain rocks.
They scoff at me by echoing what I say.

If I brought news of money, or a love-note
from a sweetheart, they'd welcome me.
But not with this prophecy-talk.

It's like a blood-soaked bandage
stuck to a sore on a donkey's back.
The one who tries to remove it
is being helpful, but also,
he's going to get kicked!

No one here wants to be healed.
Show me someone who wants what I have!"

The king began to be curious about this man.
"What is it *exactly* that you who come
as messengers have to give?"

"What do we not have!
But let's suppose for a moment that
my inspiration is not divine.

Still, you would agree, my speaking
is not *inferior* to the workings of a bee?

The *Qur'an* says, *God has inspired the bee.*
This universe is filled with honey.

Human beings feed on it and evolve upward
with the same, but more profound,
inspiration as the bee."

So the man defended his claim.
You have read about the inspired spring.

Drink from there. Be companions with those
whose lips are wet with that water.

Others, even though they may be your father
or your mother, they're your enemies.
Leave, before they kill you!

The pathless path opens
whenever you genuinely say,

*There is no Reality but God.*
*There is only God.*

(V, 1105-1151,1162,1226-1241)

54

## The Indian Tree

A learned man once said,
just for the sake of saying *something,*
"There is a tree in India.
If you eat the fruit of that tree,
you'll never grow old, and never die."

Stories about "The Tree" were passed around,
and finally a king sent his envoy to India
to look for it. People laughed at the man.
They slapped him on the back and called out,

"Sir, I know where your tree is,
but it's far in the jungle,
and you'll need a ladder!"

He kept traveling, following such directions,
and feeling foolish, for years.

He was about to return to the king,
when he met a wise man.
                              "Great teacher,
show me some kindness in this search
for the tree!"
                              "My son, this is not an actual tree,
though sometimes it has been called that.
Sometimes it's called a 'sun,' and sometimes
an 'ocean,' or a 'cloud.'
                              All these words
point to the wisdom which comes through
a True Human Being, which may have many effects,
the least of which is eternal life!

In the same way that one person can be a father
to you and a son to someone else, an uncle
to another, and a nephew to yet another,
so what you are looking for
has many names, and one existence.

Don't search for one of the names.
Move beyond any attachment to names!"

Every war, and every conflict between human beings,
has happened because of this disagreement
about *names*. It's such an unnecessary foolishness,
because just beyond the arguing,
there's a long table of companionship, set,
and waiting for us to sit down.

(II, 3641-3580)

## The Indian Parrot

There was a merchant setting out for India.

He asked each male and female servant
what they wanted to be brought as a gift.

Each told him a different exotic object:
A piece of silk, a brass figurine,
a pearl necklace.

Then he asked his beautiful caged parrot,
the one with such a lovely voice,
and she said,
        "When you see the Indian parrots,
describe my cage. Say that I need guidance
here in my separation from them. Ask how
our friendship can continue with me so confined
and them flying about freely in the meadow mist.

Tell them that I remember well our mornings
moving together from tree to tree.

Tell them to drink one cup of ecstatic wine
in honor of me here in the dregs of my life.

Tell them that the sound of their quarreling
high in the trees would be sweeter
to hear than any music."

This parrot is the spirit-bird in all of us,
that part that wants to return to freedom,
and is the freedom. What she wants
from India is *herself!*

So this parrot gave her message to the merchant,
and when he reached India, he saw a field
full of parrots. He stopped
and called out what she had told him.

One of the nearest parrots shivered
and stiffened and fell down dead.

The merchant said, "This one is surely kin
to my parrot. I shouldn't have spoken."

He finished his trading and returned home
with the presents for his workers.

When he got to the parrot, she demanded her gift.
"What happened when you told my story
to the Indian parrots?"

"I'm afraid to say."
                    "Master, you must!"

"When I spoke your complaint to the field
of chattering parrots, it broke
one of their hearts.

She must have been a close companion,
or a relative, for when she heard about you
she grew quiet and trembled, and died."

As the caged parrot heard this, she herself
quivered and sank to the cage floor.

This merchant was a good man.
He grieved deeply for his parrot, murmuring
distracted phrases, self-contradictory —
cold, then loving — clear, then
murky with symbolism.

A drowning man reaches for anything!
The Friend loves this flailing about
better than any lying still.

The One who lives inside existence
stays constantly in motion,
and whatever you do, that king
watches through the window.

When the merchant threw the "dead" parrot
out of the cage, it spread its wings
and glided to a nearby tree!

The merchant suddenly understood the mystery.
"Sweet singer, what was in the message
that taught you this trick?"

"She told me that it was the charm
of my voice that kept me caged.
*Give it up, and be released!*"

The parrot told the merchant one or two more
spiritual truths. Then a tender goodbye.

"God protect you," said the merchant
"as you go on your new way.
I hope to follow you!"

(I, 1814-1833,1845-1848)

## A Necessary Autumn Inside Each

You and I have spoken all these words,
but as for the way we have to go,
words are no preparation.

There's no getting ready,
other than grace.
My faults have stayed hidden.
One might call that a preparation!
I have one small drop of knowing in my soul.
Let it dissolve in your ocean.
There are so many threats to it.
Inside each of us, there's continual autumn.
Our leaves fall and are blown out
over the water. A crow sits
in the blackened limbs and talks
about what's gone.
                         Then your generosity
returns: spring, moisture, intelligence,
the scent of hyacinth and rose and cypress.

Joseph is back!
And if you don't feel in yourself
the freshness of Joseph,
be Jacob!

Weep, and then smile.
Don't pretend to know something
you haven't experienced.

There's a necessary dying,
and then Jesus is breathing again.

Very little grows
on jagged rock.
Be ground.

Be crumbled,
so wildflowers will come up
where you are.

You've been stony for too many years.
Try something different.
Surrender.

(I, 1878-1912)

## Your Fears of Work

Again, we hear the rhythm
between lover and Beloved, that synchrony
of drums,
           bales of sugarcane
being unloaded!
              The price goes down so far,
it's almost free. The only work
is pounding cane.
            No one leaves here
with a sour mouth! Climb the minaret,
and invite everyone to wine and dessert!
Even a nine-year-old vinegar
                 gets a sweet tinge!
Ordinary stones are suddenly
                 marbled with ruby!
All eyes feel blessed in this orchard,
and most amazingly, everyone is saying
what Hallaj said, *I am God!*

There was once a man
who rushed terrified into a house,
his face yellow, his lips blue, and his hands
trembling like an old man's.
                "What's wrong?"
"Outside! They're rounding up donkeys
to do some labor!"
              "Why are you upset?"
"They are so fierce in their purpose
that they might take me too!"
Don't be like this man.
Quit talking about your fears of work
and of being uncomfortable.

It's time to speak of roses and pomegranates,
and of the ocean where pearls are made
of language and vision, and of the invisible ladders,
which are different for each person, that lead
to the infinite place where trees

murmur among themselves,
                    "What a fine stretch
this is in the air today!"
                    And nightingales ask
the just-beginning nubs of fruit that appear
when the blossoms fall off,
                    "Give us some of what
you're drinking!"
                    Join that endless joy-talking,
and forget the other, the worrying that
you might be taken for a jackass!

                                        (V, 2525-2563)

## A Sheikh Comes Into a Tavern

A sheikh comes into a tavern saying,
"I have been fasting. Give me something to drink.
Necessity allows me this."

They brought him a cup, and he said,
"Look! This is not wine."

It was fine, golden honey.
For such a One there are no cups
full of form. It's all from the source.

Light that shines on dung
is not part of the dung.

He told one of his students,
"Get wine from the cellar,"
and the student went and tasted.
Each vat was filled with honey.

"Drunkards, what *is* this
you've been drinking?"

"My sheikh, everything
has turned to sweetness
because you came.

Change our souls
to how you are."

The whole world is made of dung and blood
and devil's piss, and yet
when a selfless one holds it,
it tastes like sweet springwater.

(II, 3410-3423)

## Feeling Drawn Again to Words

Husam, the center of my loving,
something has been boiling in me.

From our friendship the five Books of Husam
came circulating into the world.

Now I want to bring you the sixth,
to complete the *Mathnawi*.

Let light go out in six directions,
so that those who have not done
the circumambulation may do it
around this book.

Love has nothing to do with journeys
through time and space.

Love wants only to feel drawn
toward the Friend.

After that, secrets
may be told.

A secret moves toward
the knower of secrets.

Skeptics don't receive them.
What do lovers care about
being accepted or rejected?

There is an eloquence
beyond these words we use,
but we throw them into the air,

because, remember how Noah spoke discourses
for nine hundred years, and only then
did the ark begin to take form!

(VI, 1-10)

In the Name of God the Most Merciful, and the Most Compassionate.

This is the fourth journey toward home, toward where the great advantages are waiting for us. Reading it, mystics will feel very happy, as a meadow feels when it hears thunder, the good news of rain coming, as tired eyes look forward to sleeping. Joy for the spirit, health for the body. In here is what genuine devotion wants, refreshment, sweet fruit ripe enough for the pickiest picker, medicine, detailed directions on how to get to the Friend. All praise to God. Here is the way to renew connection with your soul, and rest from difficulties. The study of this book will be painful to those who feel separate from God. It will make the others grateful. In the hold of this ship is a cargo not found in the attractiveness of young women. Here is a reward for lovers of God. A full moon and an inheritance you thought you had lost are now returned to you. More hope for the hopeful, lucky finds for foragers, wonderful things thought of to do. Anticipation after depression, expanding after contraction. The sun comes out, and that light is what we give, in this book, to our spiritual descendents. Our gratitude to God holds them to us, and brings more besides. As the Andalusian poet, Adi al-Riga says,

> I was sleeping, and being comforted
> by a cool breeze, when suddenly a grey dove
> from a thicket sang and sobbed with longing,
> and reminded me of my own passion.

> I had been away from my own soul so long,
> so late-sleeping, but that dove's crying
> woke me and made me cry. *Praise*
> to all early-waking grievers!

Some go first, and others come long afterward. God blesses both and all in the line, and replaces what has been consumed, and provides for those who work the soil of helpfulness, and blesses Muhammed and Jesus and every other messenger and prophet. Amen, and may the Lord of all created beings bless you.

(Prose Prayer opening Book II)

*Green Ears*

There was a long drought. Crops dried up.
The vineyard leaves turned black.

People were gasping and dying like fish
thrown up on shore and left there.
But one man was always laughing and smiling.

A group came and asked,
"Have you no compassion for this suffering?"

He answered, "To your eyes this is a drought.
To me, it is a form of God's joy.

Everywhere in this desert I see green corn
growing waist-high, a sea-wilderness
of young ears greener than leeks.

I reach to touch them.
How could I not?

You and your friends are like Pharoah
drowning in the Red Sea of your body's blood.
Become friends with Moses, and see this other riverwater."

When you think your father is guilty of an injustice,
his face looks cruel. Joseph, to his envious brothers,
seemed dangerous. When you make peace with your father,
he will look peaceful and friendly. The whole world
is a form for truth.
                    When someone does not feel grateful
to that, the forms appear to be *as he feels*.
They mirror his anger, his greed, and his fear.
Make peace with the universe. Take joy in it.

It will turn to gold. Resurrection
will be *now*. Every moment,
a new beauty.

And never any boredom!
Instead this abundant, pouring
noise of many springs in your ears.

The tree limbs will move like people dancing,
who suddenly know what the mystical life is.

The leaves snap their fingers like they're hearing music.
They are! A sliver of a mirror shines out
from under a felt covering. Think how it will be
when the whole thing is open to the air and the sunlight!

There are some mysteries that I'm not telling you.
There's so much doubt everywhere, so many opinions
that say, "What you announce may be true
in the future, but not now."
But this form of universal truth that I see
says,
    *This is not a prediction. This is here*
*in this instant, cash in the hand!*

This reminds me of the sons of Uzayr,
who were out on the road looking for their father.
They had grown old, and their father had miraculously
grown young! They met him and asked, "Pardon us, sir,
but have you seen Uzayr? We heard that he's supposed
to be coming along this road today."

Yes, said Uzayr, "he's right behind me."
One of the sons replied, "That's good news!"

The other fell on the ground.
He had recognized his father.

"What do you mean *news!* We're already inside
the sweetness of his presence."

To your minds there is such a thing as *news,*
whereas to the inner knowing, it's all
in the middle of its happening.

To doubters, this is a pain.
To believers, it's gospel.
To the lover and the visionary,
it's life as it's being lived!

The rules of faithfulness
are just the door and the doorkeeper.

They keep the Presence from being interrupted.

Being unfaithful is like the outside of a fruit peeling.
It's dry and bitter because it's facing away from the center.
Being faithful is like the inside of the peeling,
wet and sweet. But the place for peelings
is the fire. The real Inside is beyond "sweet"
and "bitter." It's the source of deliciousness.

This can't be said. I'm drowning in it!

Turn back! And let me cleave a road through water
like Moses. This much I will say,
and leave the rest hidden:

your intellect is in fragments, like bits of gold
scattered over many matters. You must scrape them
together, so the royal stamp can be pressed into you.

Cohere, and you'll be as lovely as Samarcand
with its central market, or Damascus. Grain by grain,
collect the parts. You'll be more magnificent
than a flat coin. You'll be a cup
with carvings of the king
around the outside.

The Friend will become bread and springwater for you,
a lamp and a helper, your favorite dessert
and a glass of wine.
                    Union with that one
is grace. Gather the pieces,
so I can show you what is.

That's what talking is for,
to help us to be One. Many-ness
is having sixty different emotions.
Unity is peace, and silence.

I know I ought to be silent,
but the excitement of this keeps opening
my mouth as a sneeze or a yawn does.

Muhammed says, *I ask forgiveness seventy times a day,*
and I do the same. Forgive me. Forgive my talking
so much. But the way God makes mysteries *manifest*
quickens and keeps the flow of words in me continual.

A sleeper sleeps while his bedclothes drink in
the riverwater. The sleeper dreams of running around
looking for water and pointing in the dream to mirages,
"Water! There! There!" It's that *There!*
that keeps him asleep. *In the future, in the distance,*
those are illusions. Taste the *here* and the *now* of God.

This present-thirst is your real intelligence,
not the back-and-forth, mercurial brightness.
Discursiveness dies and gets put in the grave.

This contemplative joy does not.
Scholarly knowledge is a vertigo,
an exhausted famousness.
Listening is better.

Being a teacher is a form of desire,
a lightning-flash. Can you ride to Wahksh,
far up the Oxus River, on a streak of lightning?

Lightning is not guidance.
Lightning simply tells the clouds to weep.
Cry a little. The streak-lightning of our minds
comes so that we'll weep and long for our real lives.

A child's intellect says, "I should go to school."
But that intellect cannot teach itself.

A sick person's mind says, "Go to the doctor,"
but that doesn't cure the patient.

Some devils were sneaking up close to heaven
trying to hear the secrets, when a voice came,
"Get out of here. Go to the world. Listen
to the prophets!" Enter the house through the door.
It's not a long way. You are empty reeds,
but you can become sugarcane again,
if you'll listen to the guide.

When a handful of dirt was taken from the hoofprint
of Gabriel's horse and thrown inside the golden calf,
the calf lowed! That's what the guide can do
for you. The guide can make you *live*.

The guide will take your falcon's hood off.
Love is the falconer, your king.

Be trained by that. Never say, or think,
"I am better than...whoever."

That's what Satan thought.
Sleep in the spirit tree's peaceful shade,
and never stick your head out from that green.

(IV, 3242-3347)

## A Marriage at Daybreak

Do you know, brother, that you are a prince?
A son of Adam. And that the witch of Kabul,
who holds you with her color and her perfume,
is the world?
          Say the words, *I take refuge*
*with the Lord of the Daybreak.*

Avoid the hot breathing that keeps your tied
to her. She breathes on knots and no one
can unknot them. That's why the prophets came.

Look for those whose breath is cool.
When they breathe on knots, they loosen.

The old woman of the world has had you
in her net for sixty years. Her breathing
is the breathing of God's anger. But God's mercy
has more strength. Mercy is prior to wrath.

You must marry your soul.
That wedding is the way.
Union with the world is sickness.

But it's *hard* to be separated from these forms!
You don't have enough patience to give this up?
But how do you have enough patience
to do without God?

You can't quit drinking the earth's dark drink?
But how can you *not* drink from this other fountain?

You get restless, you say, when you don't sip
the world's fermentation. But if for one second
you saw the beauty of the clear water of God,
you'd think this other was embalming fluid.

Nearness to the Beloved is the splendor
of your life. Marry the Beloved.
Let the thorn of the ego slide from your foot.

What a relief to be empty!
Then God can live your life.

When you stay tied to mind and desire, you stumble
in the mud like a nearsighted donkey.

Keep smelling Joseph's shirt.
Don't be satisfied with borrowed light.
Let your brow and your face illuminate with union.

(IV, 3189-3240)

## The Many Wines

God has given us a dark wine so potent that,
drinking it, we leave the two worlds.

God has put into the form of hashish a power
to deliver the taster from self-consciousness.

God has made sleep so that
it erases every thought.

God made Majnun love Layla so much that
just her dog would cause confusion in him.

There are thousands of wines
that can take over our minds.

Don't think all ecstasies
are the same!

Jesus was lost in his love for God.
His donkey was drunk with barley.

Drink from the presence of saints,
not from those other jars.

Every object, every being,
is a jar full of delight.

Be a connoisseur,
and taste with caution.

Any wine will get you high.
Judge like a king, and choose the purest,

the ones unadulterated with fear,
or some urgency about "what's needed."

Drink the wine that moves you
as a camel moves when it's been untied,
and is just ambling about.

(IV,2683-2696)

*Ants Watching a Pen Writing*

Alexander the Great went toward Qaf Mountain
and saw that it was made of pure emerald
and that it had become a ring surrounding the world,
and he was amazed at the *immensity*
of God's creation.

"If you are a *mountain*, what are these others?"

Mt. Qaf replied, "They are my veins.
When God wills an earthquake, I throb
through one of them. When God says, *Enough!*,
I rest. Or it appears that I rest.
Actually, I'm always in motion."

Like the quickening energy of a medicinal ointment,
like intellect when speech is in rapid exchange,
so the Qaf Mountain intelligence flows
through this existence.

Once, a tiny ant saw a pen moving on paper
and tried to tell the mystery to another ant.

"It was so amazing how that penpoint
made beautiful pictures of basil leaves
and beds of roses and lilies."

Another ant suggested, "The real artist, though,
is the finger. The pen itself is
just an instrument."

　　　　　　　　A third ant said, "But,
consider further. Notice there's an arm above
whose strength controls the fingers . . . ."

The argument went on, up and up, until the chief ant
said,
　　　"Do not regard any accomplishment as proceeding
from any material form. All living forms become
unconscious in sleep and death. Form is
just the clothes of the spirit."

But even that wise ant neglected to say
what flowed inside *that*. He never mentioned
the existence of God, without which intelligence
and love and spirit would be inert.

So Alexander loved listening
to the wisdom of Qaf Mountain.
He wanted to hear everything!

"Explain to me about the attributes of God."

"Those qualities are too terrible
to put into language."

"Say then something that can be said
about the wonder of those."

"Look at the snow mountains.
You could travel through them for three hundred years
and still there would be snow mountains
in the distance, and snow falling
to replenish the coldness.

This vast snow-storehouse
keeps the world cool and safe
from destructive wantings.

God's coolness is greater than God's fire.
Snow mountain grace is more powerful
than desire's tropical heat,
and prior to it."

Remember this spiritual truth. It is unqualified,
and unconditional. Though the *before* and the *after*
are really one. Punishment and clemency, the same.

Did you know that already?
Don't say *yes*,
or *no*.

And don't blame a religion
for your being in-between answers.

A bird can fly in the air only
after it's born of bird-lust into a bird-body.

Let the stretcher come and take you wherever
that mercy knows you should go.

If you say *Yes, I knew,* you'll be pretending,
somewhat. And if you say *No,* that blade of No
will slam shut your window into God and behead you.

Be quiet in your confusion, and bewildered.
When you're completely empty, within
that silence, you'll be saying,
                              *Lead me.*
When you become that helpless,
God's kindness will act through you.

(IV, 3711-3754)

## Jonah's Unlit House

A child was crying with his head against
his father's coffin. "Why are they taking you
to such a terrible house? There's no carpet,
no lamp, no bread, no smell of cooking.

There's no door! No ladder leading up to the roof,
no neighbors to help out in difficulties.

We used to love to kiss you!
Why are you going where we can't?"

Juhi and his father were passing by.
Young Juhi said, "It sounds like they're taking
the corpse over to our house."
                                   "What do you mean?"
"All those things he said are true of our place."

Like that, sometimes people don't see the signs
that are so close, even how their homes
are unlit! The way you're living now is like
living in a tomb! There's none of God's light,
and no openness.
                         Remember that you're alive!
Don't stay in a narrow, choked place.
Let your Joseph out of prison!

Your Jonah has cooked long enough in the whale!
Have you forgotten what praise is?

The world is an ocean. The body, a fish.
Jonah is your soul, which cannot see the dawn,
until you glorify God like Jonah did.

Then you'll be released. There are spirit-fishes
all around you, bumping, trying to help,
but you can't see them.

Listen to their singing. Hear how they praise,
and be patient. Patience is your way to glory.

                                      **(II, 3116-3147)**

## Of Being Woven

"The Way is full of genuine sacrifice.

The thickets blocking the path are anything
that keeps you from that, any fear
that you may be broken to bits like a glass bottle.
This road demands courage and stamina,

yet it's full of footprints! Who *are*
these companions? They are rungs
in your ladder. Use them!
With company you quicken your ascent.

You may be happy enough going along,
but with others you'll get farther, and faster.

Someone who goes cheerfully by himself
to the customs house to pay his traveler's tax
will go even more lightheartedly
when friends are with him.

Every prophet sought out companions.
A wall standing alone is useless,
but put three or four walls together,
and they'll support a roof and keep
the grain dry and safe.

When ink joins with a pen, then the blank paper
can say something. Rushes and reeds must be *woven*
to be useful as a mat. If they weren't interlaced,
the wind would blow them away.

Like that, God paired up creatures,
and gave them friendship."

This is how the fowler and the bird were arguing
about hermitic living and Islam.

It's a prolonged debate.
Husam, shorten their controversy.
Make the *Mathnawi* more nimble and less lumbering.
Agile sounds are more appealing to the heart's ear.

**(VI, 507-513,517-525)**

80

## Tracks in the Nightsky

Tell me, is there any blessing
that someone's not excluded from?

What do donkeys and cows
have to do with fancy desserts?

Every soul needs different nourishment,
but be aware if your food is accidental
and habitual, or if it's something
that feeds your real nature.

It may be, like those who eat clay, that human beings
have forgotten what their original food is.
They may be feeding their diseases.

Our true food is God's light.
Animals and what animals eat
are not right for humans.

But because they are sick and dizzy, pale,
stumbling and weak, they don't hunt the game
that leaves its tracks in the nightsky.

Tasting that is done without silverware,
and without a throat. It comes down
from the throne of God. This other
is just dust kicked up from the carpet.

But we receive nourishment
from everyone we meet. Any association
is food. Planet comes near planet,
and both are affected.

Man comes together with woman,
and there's a new baby! Iron meets stone,
sparks. Rain enters the ground, and sweet herbs appear.
When green things and people converge,
there'll be laughter and dancing,
and that makes good and generous things begin.

As we move about in the open, our appetites sharpen.
Flushed faces come from the sun. That rose-red

is the most beautiful color on earth.
Through such runnings-together, the potential world
becomes actual. Live in that place of pure being.

Don't worry about having ten days of famousness here.
Revolve with me about the sun that never sets.
Work cannot be separated from the Worker.

(II, 1077-1116)

## Wealth Without Working

In the time of David there was a man
who used to pray out loud,
                              "Lord, give me wealth
without working! You created me lazy and slow,
so let me have my daily bread by being just that.

Pay me for sleeping in the shade! It's your shade.
Give me sudden riches with no fatigue on my part.
Let this prayer be all that I do."

He prayed this way before a wise teacher,
or in front of the town simpleton.

It made no difference who was listening.
He prayed day and night, every day.

People laughed at him, of course.
"This weak-bearded idiot!"
                              "Did someone give him
some hashish?"
                      "Livelihood comes with effort,
but this guy says, 'I will climb up into the sky
without a ladder.'"
                        "Oh sir, the messenger has come
with the news you've been waiting for!"
                                          "Could I have
a little part of what you get from this prayer?"

So it went. But nothing made him stop. He became famous
for being the one who keeps looking for cheese
in an empty food pouch. He was a living proverb
on foolishness.
                    Then one morning, suddenly,
a large cow walked into his house. With her horns
she broke the lock and butted the bolt back
and came in!
                  The man quit praying. He bound
the cow's legs, cut her throat, and ran
to get the butcher. There was enough food
and leather for a long time!

Do that for me, You who make demands like an embryo
growing inside me. Help me with this long poem!

You're asking for gold. First, give me gold in secret.
All these images and words have to come from You.

Everyone, and every thing, and every action, glorifies
You, but sometimes the way one does it
is not recognized by another.

Human beings rarely understand how inanimate objects
are doing it, the walls and the doors and the rocks,
those masters of glorification!

We squabble over the doctrines of the Sunnis
and the Jabris, and all their seventy-two
different interpretations. It never ends.

But we don't hear the inanimate objects
speaking to each other, and to us!

How can we understand the praising
of what doesn't speak?

Only with the help of the One whose love
opens into the spirit's telling.

(III, 1450-1464,1479-1509)

## The Trick About Thawing Grapes

I speak harshly to free you from meanness,
as frozen grapes thaw with pouring *cold* water
on them. That loosens the hardness and bitterness.

With a little scolding, you warm,
and the sweet grape-blood comes back.

**(III, 4193-4196)**

*Turning Toward Kindness*

Anyone who genuinely and constantly with both hands
looks for something, will find it.

Though you are lame and bent over, keep moving
toward the Friend. With speech, with silence,
with sniffing about, stay on the track.

Whenever some kindness comes to you, turn
that way, toward the source of kindness.

Love-things originate in the ocean.
Restlessness leads to rest.

(III, 978-981,987-992)

In the Name of God, the Merciful and Compassionate.

The start of the second book of the *Mathnawi* has been postponed, and the reason is this: Sometimes God reveals *all* the wisdom of doing a certain action, and the listener becomes so overwhelmed in contemplating that, that he is unable to perform it. Lost in the infinity, with no ability to understand, or *do,* anything.

God then reduces the wisdom portion, and makes a small bridle to fit over the listener's head to lead him by. The size of the bridle is important when you're dealing with a stubborn camel. Too heavy, and he'll lie down and refuse to move. Too slight, and he'll ignore it. The proportion of wisdom to personal advantage is a subtle mixture, like that of clay and water to make bricks. Too little water, and it won't cohere. Too much, and it washes away. God gives attention to an individual's balance, except when giving to those described in the text, *He gives, and they receive without calculating.* But that state cannot be understood without tasting it.

Someone once asked, "What is love?"

"Be lost in me," I said. "You'll know love when that happens."

Love has no calculating in it. That's why it's said to be a quality of God and not of human beings. God loves you is the only possible sentence. The subject becomes the object so totally that it can't be turned around. Who will the "you" pronoun stand for, if you say, "You love God" ?

(Prose Preface to Book II)

87

*Emptiness*

Consider the difference
in our actions and God's actions.

We often ask, "Why did you do that?"
or "Why did I act like that?"

We *do* act, and yet everything we do
is God's creative action.

We look back and analyze the events
of our lives, but there is another way
of seeing, a backward-and-forward-at-once
vision, that is not rationally understandable.

Only God can understand it.
Satan made the excuse, *You caused me to fall,*
whereas Adam said to God, *We did this
to ourselves.* After this repentence,
God asked Adam, *Since all is within
my foreknowledge, why didn't you
defend yourself with that reason?*

Adam answered, *I was afraid,
and I wanted to be reverent.*

Whoever acts with respect will get respect.
Whoever brings sweetness will be served almond cake.
Good women are drawn to be with *good* men.

Honor your friend.
Or treat him rudely,
and see what happens!

Love, tell an incident now
that will clarify this mystery
of how we act freely, and are yet
compelled. One hand shakes with palsy.
Another shakes because you slapped it away.

Both tremblings come from God,
but you feel guilty for the one,
and what about the other?

These are intellectual questions.
The spirit approaches the matter
differently. Omar once had a friend, a scientist,
Bu'l-Hakam, who was flawless at solving
empirical problems, but he could not follow Omar
into the area of illumination and wonder.

Now I return to the text, "And He is with you,
wherever you are," but when have I ever left it!

Ignorance is God's prison.
Knowing is God's palace.

We sleep in God's unconsciousness.
We wake in God's open hand.

We weep God's rain.
We laugh God's lightning.

Fighting and peacefulness
both take place within God.

Who are we then
in this complicated world-tangle,
that is really just the single, straight
line down at the beginning of *ALLAH*?

Nothing.
We are
emptiness.

(I, 1480-1514)

## I Have Five Things To Say

The wakened lover speaks directly to the Beloved,
"You are the sky my spirit circles in,
the love inside love, the resurrection-place.

Let this window be your ear.
I have lost consciousness many times
with longing for your listening silence,
and your life-quickening smile.

You give attention to the smallest matters,
my suspicious doubts, and to the greatest.

You know my coins are counterfeit,
but You accept them anyway,
my impudence and my pretending!

I have five things to say,
five fingers to give
into your grace.

First, when I was apart from You,
        this world did not exist,
            nor any other.

Second, whatever I was looking for
            was always You.

Third, why did I ever learn to count to three?

Fourth, my cornfield is burning!

Fifth, this finger stands for Rabia,
            and this is for someone else.
            Is there a difference?

Are these words or tears?
Is weeping speech?
What shall I do, my love?"

So he speaks, and everyone around
begins to cry with him, laughing crazily,
moaning in the spreading union
of lover and Beloved.

This is the true religion. All others
are thrown-away bandages beside it.

This is the *sema* of slavery and mastery
dancing together. This is not-being.

Neither words, nor any natural fact
can express this.

I know these dancers.
Day and night I sing their songs
in this phenomenal cage.

My soul, don't try to answer now!
Find a friend, and hide.

But what can stay hidden?
Love's secret is always lifting its head
out from under the covers,
"Here I am!"

(III, 4694-4734)

## The Seed Market

Can you find another market like this?

Where,
with your one rose
you can buy hundreds of rose gardens?

Where,
for one seed
you get a whole wilderness?

For one weak breath,
the divine wind?

You've been fearful
of being absorbed in the ground,
or drawn up by the air.

Now, your waterbead lets go
and drops into the ocean,
where it came from.

It no longer has the form it had,
but it's still water.
The essence is the same.

This giving up is not a repenting.
It's a deep honoring of yourself.

When the ocean comes to you as a lover,
marry, at once, quickly,
for God's sake!

Don't postpone it!
Existence has no better gift.

No amount of searching
will find this.

A perfect falcon, for no reason,
has landed on your shoulder,
and become yours.

(IV, 2611-2625)

## Birdsong from Inside the Egg

Sometimes a lover of God may faint
in the presence. Then the Beloved bends
and whispers in his ear, "Beggar, spread out
your robe. I'll fill it with gold.

I've come to protect your consciousness.
Where has it gone? Come back into awareness!"

This fainting is because
lovers want *so much.*

A chicken invites a camel into her hen-house,
and the whole structure is demolished.

A rabbit nestles down
with its eyes closed
in the arms of a lion.

There is an *excess*
in spiritual searching
that is profound ignorance.

Let that ignorance be our teacher!
The Friend breathes into one
who has no breath.

A deep silence revives the listening
and the speaking of those two
who meet on the riverbank.

Like the ground turning green in a spring wind.
Like birdsong beginning inside the egg.

Like this universe coming into existence,
the lover wakes, and whirls
in a dancing joy,

then kneels down
in praise.

(III, 4664-4693)

## Body Intelligence

Your intelligence is always with you,
overseeing your body, even though
you may not be aware of its work.

If you start doing something against
your health, your intelligence
will eventually scold you.

If it hadn't been so lovingly close by,
and so constantly monitoring,
how could it rebuke?

You and your intelligence
are like the beauty and the precision
of an astrolabe.

Together, you calculate how near
existence is to the sun!

Your intelligence is marvelously intimate.
It's not in front of you or behind,
or to the left or the right.

Now try, my friend, to describe how near
is the creator of your intellect!

Intellectual searching will not find
the way to that king!

The movement of your finger
is not separate from your finger.

You go to sleep, or you die,
and there's no intelligent motion.

Then you wake,
and your fingers
fill with meanings.

Now consider the jewel-lights
in your eyes. How do *they* work?

This visible universe has many weathers

and variations.
　　　　　　But uncle, O uncle,
the universe of the creation-word,
the divine command to *Be,* that universe
of qualities is beyond any pointing-to.

More intelligent than intellect,
and more spiritual than spirit.
No being is unconnected
to that reality, and that connection
cannot be said. *There,* there's
no separation and no return.

There are guides who can show you the way.
Use them. But they will not satisfy your longing.

Keep wanting that connection
with all your pulsing energy.

The throbbing vein
will take you farther
than any thinking.

Muhammed said, *"Don't theorize
about Essence!"* All speculations
*are* just more layers of covering.
Human beings love coverings!

They think the designs on the curtains
are what's being concealed.

Observe the wonders as they occur around you.
Don't claim them. Feel the artistry
moving through, and be silent.

Or say, "I cannot praise You
as You should be praised.

Such words are infinitely
beyond my understanding."

(IV, 3678-3703,3708-3710)

## Humble and Active

The saying, *Whatever God wills, will happen,*
does not end, "Therefore be passive."

Rather, it means, *Forget yourself,*
*and get ready to help.*

If you were told that whatever you wished for
would come into being, and then if you neglected
to do something, there would be no problem,
because it would happen, somehow, anyway.

But instead, you are told
that whatever God wills, will happen.

Stay alert then, and close by,
like a worker waiting to perform
whatever needs to be done.

Your attitude has been a reverse
interpretation of the text.

The way you distinguish a true commentary
from a false is this:
                Whichever explication
makes you feel fiery and hopeful, humble
and *active,* that's the true one.

If it makes you lazy, it's not right.

Ask the *Qur'an* about the *Qur'an.*
Ask the *Bible* about the *Bible,*
not some burnt-out intellectual.

Or ask someone who has disappeared
into the essence within the writing.

There is an oil that's
totally saturated with roses.

Smell that, or
the roses, whichever.

(V, 3111-3130)

## Joy at Sudden Disappointment

Whatever comes, comes from a need,
a *sore distress*, a hurting want.

Mary's pain made the baby Jesus.
Her womb opened its lips
and spoke the Word.

Every part of you has a secret language.
Your hands and your feet say what you've done.

And every need brings in what's needed.
Pain bears its cure like a child.

Having nothing produces provisions.
Ask a difficult question,
and the marvelous answer appears.

Build a ship, and there'll be water
to float it. The tender-throated
infant cries and milk drips
from the mother's breast.

Be thirsty for the ultimate water,
and then be ready for what will
come pouring from the spring.

A village woman once was walking by Muhammed.
She thought he was just an ordinary illiterate.
She didn't believe that he was a prophet.

She was carrying a two-months old baby.
As she came near Muhammed, the baby turned
and said, "Peace be with you, Messenger of God."

The mother cried out, surprised and angry,
"What are you saying,
and how can you suddenly talk!"

The child replied, "God taught me first,
and then Gabriel."
                    "Who is this Gabriel?
I don't see anyone."

"He is above your head,
mother. Turn around. He has been telling me
many things."
            "Do you really see him?"
                                "Yes.
He is continually delivering me from this
degraded state into sublimity."

Muhammed then asked the child,
"What is your name?"

"Abdul Aziz, the servant of God, but this family
thinks I am concerned with world-energies.
I am as free of that as the truth of your prophecy is."

So the little one spoke, and the mother
took in a fragrance that let her surrender
to that state.
            When God gives this knowing,
inanimate stones, plants, animals, everything,
fills with unfolding significance.

The fish and the birds become protectors.
Remember the incident of Muhammed and the eagle.

It happened that as he was listening
to this inspired baby, he heard a voice
calling him to prayer. He asked for water
to perform ablutions. He washed his hands
and feet, and just as he reached for his boot,

an eagle snatched it away! The boot turned upsidedown
as it lifted, and a poisonous snake dropped out.

The eagle circled and brought the boot back,
saying, "My helpless reverence for you
made this necessary. Anyone who acts
this presumptuously for a legalistic reason
should be punished!"
                    Muhammed thanked the eagle,
and said, "What I thought was rudeness
was really love. You took away my grief,
and I was grieved! God has shown me everything,

but at that moment I was preoccupied within myself."
The eagle,
          "But Chosen One, any clarity I have
comes from you!"
                    This spreading radiance
of a True Human Being has great importance.

Look carefully around you and recognize
the luminosity of souls. Sit beside those
who draw you to that.
                    Learn from this eagle story
that when misfortune comes, you must quickly praise.

Others may be saying, *Oh no,* but you
will be opening out like a rose
losing itself petal by petal.

Someone once asked a great sheikh
what sufism was.
                    "The feeling of joy
when sudden disappointment comes."

The eagle carries off Muhammed's boot
and saves him from snakebite.

Don't grieve for what doesn't come.
Some things that don't happen
keep disasters from happening.

                                        (III, 3204-3265)

99

## A Sunrise Ruby

In the early morning hour,
just before dawn, lover and Beloved wake
and take a drink of water.

She asks, "Do you love me or yourself more?
Really, tell the absolute truth."

He says, "There's nothing left of *me*.
I'm like a ruby held up to the sunrise.
Is it still a stone, or a world
made of redness? It has no resistance
to sunlight."

This is how Hallaj said, *I am God,*
and told the truth!

The ruby and the sunrise are one.
Be courageous and discipline yourself.

Completely become hearing and ear,
and wear this sun-ruby as an earring.

Work. Keep digging your well.
Don't think about getting off from work.
Water is there somewhere.

Submit to a daily practice.
Your loyalty to that
is a ring on the door.

Keep knocking, and the joy inside
will eventually open a window
and look out to see who's there.

(V, 2020-2049)

## Love is the Whirlpool's Energy

Being a lover
and feeling patient and repentent
do not go together.

Love is a dragon.
Being ashamed is a little worm.

One is a quality of God.
The other, an emotion full of thinking.

Love is moonlight on your bedroom wall,
the energy of a whirlpool.

When it's not there,
a human being becomes a frantic
fish at the bottom of the place
where the whirlpool was,

or just a blank barrier between sleepers.

**(VI, 969-983)**

## Don't Postpone Your Yes!

Muhammed is said to have said,
"Whoever belongs to God, God belongs to."

Our weak, uneven breathings,
these dissolving personalities,
were breathed out by the eternal
*Huuuuuuu,* that never changes!

A drop of water constantly fears
that it may evaporate into air,
or be absorbed by the ground.

It doesn't want to be used up
in those ways, but when it lets go
and falls into the ocean it came from,
it finds protection from the other deaths.

Its droplet form is gone,
but its watery essence has become
vast and inviolable.

Listen to me, friends, because *you*
are a drop, and you can honor yourselves
in this way. What could be luckier

than to have the ocean come
to court the drop?

For God's sake, don't postpone your *yes!*
Give up and become the giver.

(IV, 2613-2622)

## Singular & Plural

As human beings have an intellect
beyond the animals, so True Human Beings

have an intelligent soul
beyond ordinary awareness,

and it is all one thing,
their knowing and doing.

David didn't build the temple.
His son Solomon did,
but David built it too!

We speak of saints and prophets
and awakened ones in the plural,
but that's not the way it is.

Dogs and wolves are competitive and disparate,
but the lions of God have one soul.

(IV, 406–415)

## Dhu'l-Nun's Instructive Madness

Some friends of Dhu'l-Nun, the Egyptian,
went to see about him. They had heard
that he had gone spectacularly insane,

that he was a wildfire no one could contain,
this man who had been such a source of wisdom.

They arrived at his house. He yelled, "Hey,
you'd better watch out coming here.
Who are you?"
                    "Don't you remember us?
We're your friends! What secret
are you hiding with this madness?"

Dhu'l-Nun began to rave a mixture
of filthy language and gibberish.

He rushed out and grabbed up stones
and threw them at the group. They ran.

"See!" he called. "You're not friends.
A friend does not run away from pain
inflicted by a friend.

There's a joy within suffering
that is the kernel of friendship.

A friend is pure gold singing
inside the refining fire.

He thrives on fights and misunderstandings,
and even madness."

(II, 1386-1387,1430-1432,1447-1461)

## Kings with their Wooden Sticks

A group of kings were arguing
with Muhammed.
              "You are a king as we are,
but you do not acknowledge our power.

Share your kingdom with us, as we divide
the sovereignty of the world among ourselves."

"God has given differently to you
than he has to me."
              And with that a cloud came,
and it rained down a terrible flood.

The kings threw their sceptres at the water,
and those symbols of authority were swept away
like bits of straw.
              Then the Prophet threw his staff,
and it stood up on the flood like a sentry,
and the water subsided and became gentle.

The kings bowed and confessed their failings
to the Prophet, all except for three of them,
who thought that it was some occult trick.

Whenever you wonder how prophetic majesty
differs from political kingship, remember
these wooden sticks lost in the floodwater
like so many forgotten potentates.

Then remember Muhammed's calming presence,
that's still here.

(IV, 2779-2800)

## Craftsmanship and Emptiness

I've said before that every craftsman
searches for what's not there
to practice his craft.

A builder looks for the rotten hole
where the roof caved in. A water-carrier
picks the empty pot. A carpenter
stops at the house with no door.

Workers rush toward some hint
of emptiness, which they then
start to fill. Their hope, though,
is for emptiness, so don't think
you must avoid it. It contains
what you need!
                    Dear soul, if you were not friends
with the vast nothing inside,
why would you always be casting your net
into it, and waiting so patiently?

This invisible ocean has given you such abundance,
but still you call it "death,"
that which provides you sustenance and work.

God has allowed some magical reversal to occur,
so that you see the scorpion pit
as an object of desire,
and all the beautiful expanse around it
as dangerous and swarming with snakes.

This is how strange your fear of death
and emptiness is, and how perverse
the attachment to what you want.

Now that you've heard me
on your misapprehensions, dear friend,
listen to Attar's story on the same subject.

He strung the pearls of this
about King Mahmud, how among the spoils
of his Indian campaign there was a Hindu boy,

whom he adopted as a son. He educated
and provided royally for the boy
and later made him vice-regent, seated
on a gold throne beside himself.

One day he found the young man weeping.
"Why are you crying? You're the companion
of an emperor! The entire nation is ranged out
before you like stars that you can command!"

The young man replied, "I am remembering
my mother and my father, and how they
scared me as a child with threats of you!
'Uh-oh, he's headed for King Mahmud's court!
Nothing could be more hellish!' Where are they now
when they should see me sitting here?"

This incident is about your fear of changing.
You are the Hindu boy. *Mahmud,* which means,
*Praise to the End,* is the spirit's
poverty, or emptiness.

The mother and father are your attachment
to beliefs and bloodties
and desires and comforting habits.

Don't listen to them!
They seem to protect,
but they imprison.

They are your worst enemies.
They make you afraid
of living in emptiness.

Some day you'll weep tears of delight in that court,
remembering your mistaken parents!

Know that your body nurtures the spirit,
helps it grow, and then gives it wrong advice.

The body becomes, eventually, like a vest
of chainmail in peaceful years,
too hot in summer and too cold in winter.

But the body's desires, in another way, are like
an unpredictable associate, whom you must be
patient with. And that companion is helpful,
because patience expands your capacity
to love and feel peace.

The patience of a rose close to a thorn
keeps it fragrant. It's patience that gives milk
to the male camel still nursing in its third year,
and patience is what the prophets show to us.

The beauty of careful sewing on a shirt
is the patience it contains.

Friendship and loyalty have patience
as the strength of their connections.

Feeling lonely and ignoble indicates
that you haven't been patient.

Be with those who mix with God
as honey blends with milk, and say,

"Anything that comes and goes,
rises and sets, is not
what I love."

Live in the One who created the prophets,
else you'll be like a caravan fire left
to flare itself out alone beside the road.

(VI, 1369-1420)

## The Granary Floor

A sufi was wandering the world.
One night he came as a guest to a community of sufis.
He tied up his donkey in the stable
and then was welcomed to the head of the dais.
They went into deep meditation and mystical communion,
he and these friends. For such people
a person's presence is more to learn from
than a book. A sufi's book is not composed
with ink and alphabet. A scholar loves, and lives on,
the marks of a pen. A sufi loves footprints!
He sees those and stalks his game. At first, he *sees*
the clues. After a time he can follow the scent.
To go guided by fragrance is a hundred times better
than following tracks. A person who is opening
to the divine is like a door to a sufi.
What might appear a worthless stone
to others, to him's a pearl. You see your image
clearly in a mirror. A sheikh sees more than that
in a discarded brick. Sufi masters are those
whose spirits existed before the world.
Before the body, they lived many lifetimes.

Before seeds went into the ground, they harvested wheat.
Before there was an ocean, they strung pearls.
While the great meeting was going on about bringing
human beings into existence, they stood up to their chins
in wisdom water. When some of the angels opposed
creation, the sufi sheikhs laughed and clapped
among themselves. Before materiality, they knew
what it was like to be trapped inside matter.
Before there was a nightsky, they saw Saturn.
Before wheatgrains, they tasted bread.
With no mind, they thought.

Immediate intuition to them is the simplest act
of consciousness, what to others would be epiphany.
Much of our thought is of the past, or the future.
They're free of those. Before a mine is dug,

they judge coins. Before vineyards,
they know the excitements to come.
In July, they feel December.
In unbroken sunlight, they find shade. In *fana,*
the state where all objects dissolve,
they recognize objects. The open sky drinks
from their circling cup. The sun wears
the gold of their generosity.

When two of them meet, they are no longer two.
They are one and six hundred thousand.

The ocean waves are their closest likeness,
when wind makes from unity, the numerous.
This happened to the sun, and it broke into rays
through the window, into bodies.
The disc of the sun does exist, but if you see
only the ray-bodies, you may have doubts.
The human-divine combination is a oneness.
Plurality, the apparent separation into rays.

Friend, we're traveling together.
Throw off your tiredness. Let me show you
one tiny spot of the beauty that cannot be spoken.
I'm like an ant that's gotten into the granary,
ludicrously happy, and trying to lug out
a grain that's way too big.

(II, 156-193)

## What Is a Lover?

One who has no motive,
as he gambles everything, doing what
is not part of any religion.

No ordinary madness, this.
If it came over a doctor, he would blur
his medical books with tears.

All medicines are just images
of the loving of the lover,

whose face looks inward,
with no kin but the one You.

The pointer of the prayer rug turns
on its center, where you kneel.

Call out *Lord,* and hear
within that, *Am I not . . . ?*

(VI, 1969-1987)

## *What is the Path?*

A self-sacrificing way,
but also a warrior's way, and not
for brittle, easily-broken, glass-bottle people.

The soul is tested here by sheer terror,
as a sieve sifts and separates
genuine from fake.

And this road is full of footprints!
Companions have come before.
They are your ladder.
Use them!

Without them you won't have the spirit-quickness
you need. Even a dumb donkey
crossing a desert becomes nimblefooted
with others of its kind.

Stay with a caravan. By yourself,
you'll get a hundred times more tired,
and fall behind.

(VI, 507-513)

## After the Meditation

Now I see something in my listeners
that won't let me continue this way.

The ocean flows back in
and puts up a foam barrier,
and then withdraws.

After a while,
it will come in again.

This audience wants to hear more
about the visiting sufi and his friends
in meditation. But be discerning.

Don't think of this as a normal character
in an ordinary story.

The ecstatic meditation ended.
Dishes of food were brought out.
The sufi remembered his donkey
that had carried him all day.

He called to the servant there, "Please,
go to the stable and mix the barley generously
with the straw for the animal. Please."

"Don't worry yourself with such matters.
All things have been attended to."

"But I want to make sure that you wet the barley first.
He's an old donkey, and his teeth are shakey."
"Why are you telling me this?
I have given the appropriate orders."

"But did you remove the saddle gently,
and put salve on the sore he has?"

"I have served thousands of guests
with these difficulties, and all have gone away
satisfied. Here, you are treated as family.
Do not worry. Enjoy yourself."

"But did you warm his water
just a little, and then add only a bit of straw
to the barley?"
                    "Sir, I'm ashamed for you."
                                        "And please,
sweep the stall clean of stones and dung,
and scatter a little dry earth in it."

"For God's sake, sir,
leave my business to *me!*"

"And did you currycomb his back?
He loves that."
                    "Sir! I am *personally*
responsible for all these chores!"

The servant turned and left at a brisk pace . . .
to join his friends in the street.

The sufi then lay down to sleep
and had terrible dreams about his donkey,
how it was being torn to pieces by a wolf,
or falling helplessly into a ditch.

And his dreaming was right! His donkey
was being totally neglected, weak and gasping,
without food or water all the night long.
The servant had done nothing he said he would.

There are such vicious and empty flatterers
in your life. Do the careful,
donkey-tending work.

Don't trust that to anyone else.
There are hypocrites who will praise you,
but who do not care about the health
of your heart-donkey.
                    Be concentrated and *leonine*
in the hunt for what is your true nourishment.
Don't be distracted by blandishment-noises,
of any sort.

(II, 194-223,260-263)

## The Dog in the Doorway

This is how it is when your animal-energies,
the *nafs*, dominate your soul:

You have a piece of fine linen
that you're going to make into a coat
to give to a friend, but someone else uses it
to make a pair of pants. The linen
has no choice in the matter.
It must submit. Or, it's like
someone breaks in your house
and goes to the garden and plants thornbushes.
An ugly humiliation falls over the place.

Or, you've seen a nomad's dog
lying at the tent entrance, with his head
on the threshold and his eyes closed.

Children pull his tail and touch his face,
but he doesn't move. He loves the children's
attention and stays humble within it.

But if a stranger walks by, he'll spring up
ferociously. Now, what if that dog's owner
were not able to control it?

A poor dervish might appear: the dog storms out.
The dervish says, "I take refuge with God
when the dog of arrogance attacks,"
and the owner has to say, "So do I!
I'm helpless against this creature
even in my own house!

Just as you can't come close,
I can't go out!"

This is how animal-energy becomes monstrous
and ruins your life's freshness and beauty.

Think of taking this dog
out to hunt! You'd be the quarry.

(V, 2922-2928,2940-2943,2956-2962)

## Opening

Someone asked a preacher once,
"If a bird lands on the city wall,
which is more admirable, its head
or its tail?"
         He answered according to
what the man was ready to hear.
                "If it's facing in,
toward the community, the head, but if it's turned
toward the desert, even the bits of dust
on its tail are better. Intention is everything."

A lover may look murky with good and evil actions,
but consider only his aspirations. A falcon
may appear elegantly fierce, but watch
when it sees a mouse. There are owls
who desire more the forearm of the king.
Don't judge by any outward, hooded form.

Some human beings no bigger than a water trough
scooped out of a log are greater glories
than the universe full of stars.

*We have honored you,* says the *Qur'an.*
A grieving human being heard that from God!

The beauty and elegance and clarity and love
that we have deserve to be offered into
regions higher than this visible one.

Are you friendly with pictures
on the bath-house wall? No.
You walk out of there and talk
to a half-blind old woman.

What's in her that's not in the pictures?
I'll tell you. Discernment and soul.

In a *living* old blind woman
there's a mixing of body and spirit.

What is the soul? A joy
when kindness comes, a weeping
at injury, a growing consciousness.

The more awareness one has
the closer to God he or she is.

There are definite levels of soul.
The first is phenomenal, a play put on
in the courtyard, mingling human and divine.

What happens in the inner essence
of soul is the theatre of God!

Angels were considered entirely ethereal,
until Adam. Then the angels seemed
denser than that human being.

They bowed to it, all but Satan.
He was like a broken hand that doesn't respond
to the body's spirit. The spirit itself
is not broken, just the dead limb,
and it can be brought to life again.

There are more mysteries to be told,
but who will hear?

Certain parrots eat a profound candy.
Others close their eyes and turn away.

Soul-reality is not just metrical feet
and clever rhyming. Someone who looks
like a dervish may not be one.

There is a Seal on the mouth that unseals,
locks long unopened that loosen
with *We have opened you.*

"Show the way" in this world becomes
"Show them the moon" in the other.

Both gates are opening now.
The Seal is the opener of seals,
as when you say of a master of some craft,
"They broke the mould with you."

It's revelation within revelation within
revelation, a generous giving of soul-growth.

In Baghdad, or Herat, or Rayy, it doesn't matter,
the rosebranch blossoms the same rose many times.

The wine jars bubble the same wine all over town.
Light in the west or from the east,
it's the same sun.

(VI, 129-179)

## Die Before You Die

Love's sun is the face of the Friend.
This other sunlight is covering that.

The day and the daily bread that comes
are not to be worshipped for themselves.

Praise the great heart within those,
and the loving ache in yourself
that's part of that.

Be one of God's fish
who receives what it needs
directly from the ocean around it —
food, shelter, sleep, medicine.

The lover is like a baby at its mother's breast,
knowing nothing of the visible or invisible
worlds. Everything is milk,

though it couldn't define it intellectually.
It can't talk!

This is the riddle
that drives the spirit crazy:
that the opener and that which is opened
are the same!
                    That it's the ocean *inside* the fish
bearing it along, not the riverwater.

The time-river spreads and disappears
into the ocean with the fish.

A seed breaks open and dissolves
in the ground. Only then
does a new fig tree come into being.

That's the meaning
of *Die before you die*.

(VI, 4044-4053)

## Ayaz' Work Clothes

Ayaz, the slave of God, said this
to King Mahmud about the power
of Bestami's surrender:
                    "One drop of that
could absorb an ocean, as whole forests
disappear in one spark, as some false
ego-fantasy in a king destroys
his entire army,
                    as Muhammed's star rose
and Zoroasterianism sank away.

But these images are makeshift and temporary.
No *thing* can describe Bestami's particle
of the divine. If I call it 'the sun,'
I have purposes that must stay hidden
from you, Mahmud, with your love
of worldly kingdoms.

The foam blowing on the sand
no longer understands
the pull of the ocean."

"Tell then," said King Mahmud, "about your workshoes
and the old sheepskin jacket
that you show such reverence for.

Your faith and your slavery have blended
into such a profound and mysterious beauty
that you make us free people want to be slaves!"

Ayaz explained about the shoes: "Muhammed said,
*Whoever knows himself, knows God.*

When I bow to those shoes and that jacket,
I see what the world has given me,
this body of worn and useful clothes.

Anything else I am is a gift from God.
Those work clothes help me remember
the nakedness that wears the body."

                    (V, 3393-3402,3351-3355,2113-2115)

120

## Whatever You See You Become

Shiites in Aleppo
gather at the city gate
on a certain day to remember
the Prophet's grandson, Husayn, and those
who died at the battle of Karbala.
The desert fills with mourning sounds.

A stranger, a poet, comes along.
He knows nothing of this custom.

"Someone very important
must have died!"
                    "Are you mad?"
screams one of the crowd. "This is the day
when we mourn for a single soul greater
than whole generations!"

The poet replied, "So one of the royal human beings
has escaped from prison! Why mourn? Husayn
and his family have gone to Muhammed.

If you truly know that, why aren't you ecstatic?
If you've seen the river nearby,
don't be stingy with your water."

An ant drags its one grain fearfully, blind
to the vastness of the threshing floor it walks on.
The owner of the harvest looks down at the trembling ant.

"Hey, how about this grain over here, or this?
Why are you so devoted to that particular one?"

This is how we are before we realize
that we are not this body.

Look at Saturn, lame ant. Look at
Solomon! You become what you behold.

A human being is essentially a spiritual eye.
The skin and bones fall away.
Whatever you really see, you are that.

(VI, 777-812)

121

## Dervishes

You've heard descriptions
of the ocean of non-existence.

Try, continually, to give yourself
into that ocean. Every workshop
has its foundations set
on that emptiness.

The Master of all masters
works with nothing.

The more nothing comes into your work,
the more God is there.

Dervishes gamble everything. They lose,
and win the Other, the emptiness
which animates this.

We've talked so much! Remember
what we haven't said.

And keep working. Exert yourself
toward the pull of God.

Laziness and disdain are not devotions.
Your efforts will bring a result.

You'll watch the wings of divine attraction
lift from the nest and come toward you!

As dawn lightens, blow out the candle.
Dawn is in your eyes now.

**(VI, 1466-1482)**

*Breadmaking*

There was a feast. The king
was heartily in his cups.

He saw a learned scholar walking by.
"Bring him in, and give him
some of this fine wine."

Servants rushed out and brought the man
to the king's table, but he was not
receptive. "I had rather drink poison!
I have never tasted wine and never will!
Take it away from me!"

He kept on with these loud refusals,
disturbing the atmosphere of the feast.

This is how it sometimes is
at God's table.

Someone who has *heard* about ecstatic love,
but never tasted it, disrupts the banquet.

If there were a secret passage
from his ear to his throat, everything
in him would change. Initiation would occur.

As it is, he's all fire and no light,
all husk and no kernel.

The king gave orders. "Cupbearer,
do what you must!"

This is how your invisible guide acts,
the chess champion across from you
that always wins. He cuffed
the scholar's head and said,
                    "Taste!"
And, "Again!"
                The cup was drained,
and the intellectual started singing
and telling ridiculous jokes.

He joined the garden, snapping his fingers
and swaying. Soon, of course,
he had to pee.

He went out, and there, near the latrine,
was a beautiful woman, one of the king's harem.

His mouth hung open. He wanted her!
Right then, he wanted her!
And she was not unwilling.

They fell to, on the ground.
You've seen a baker rolling dough.
He kneads it gently at first,
then more roughly.

He pounds it on the board.
It softly groans under his palms.
Now he spreads it out
and rolls it flat.

Then he bunches it,
and rolls it all the way out again,
thin. Now he adds water,
and mixes it well.

Now salt,
and a little more salt.

Now he shapes it delicately
to its final shape,
then slides it into the oven,
which is already hot.

You remember breadmaking!
This is how your desire
tangles with a desired one.

And it's not just a metaphor
for a man and a woman making love.

Warriors in battle do like this too.
A great mutual embrace is always happening
between the eternal and what dies,

between essence and accident.

The sport has different rules
in every case, but it's basically
the same, and remember:

the way you make love is the way
God will be with you.

So these two were lost in their sexual trance.
They did not care anymore about feasting
or wine. Their eyes were closed like
perfectly matching calligraphy lines.

The king went looking for the scholar,
and when he saw them there coupled, commented,

"Well, as it is said, 'A good king
must serve his subjects from his own table!'"

There is joy, a wine-like freedom
that dissolves the mind and restores
the spirit, and there's a manly fortitude
like the king's, a reasonableness
that accepts the bewildered lostness.

But meditate now on steadfastness
and clarity, and let those be the wings
that lift and soar through the celestial spheres.

(VI, 3914-3979)

# Notes

"Snow and the Voice"(p. 16) — Rumi often mentions the reality of a helpful in-knowing. Sometimes he calls it "the voice," sometimes a kind of "magnetism," a being-drawn together that friends feel. The *abdals*, ("Work in the Invisible") are another level of helpers. Rumi is always clear about the collaborative nature of any action. Many beings, visible and invisible, are involved in what we do, an entire community.

"This We Have Now"(p. 22) — All of Jelaluddin Rumi's poetry comes from work within a community. In this particular segment the group has stayed up in an all-night vigil, so that the dawn itself becomes an image of the state of awareness they have reached, which is called splendor, and friendship, and "the truth that Hallaj spoke." Al-Hallaj Mansour is the sufi mystic martyred in Baghdad in 922 for saying *An al-Haqq*, or "I am the truth," or "I am God." The ineffable inner majesty celebrated here ("What else could human beings want?") is *prior* to the existence of the universe and, Rumi asserts in many places, the *seed* that it grew from.

"Dhu'l-Nun's Instructive Madness,"(p. 104) — Dhu'l-Nun (796-859) was an Egyptian sufi, a Nubian freedman, with a great knowledge of alchemy. He is thought to be a link to the spiritual sciences of ancient Egypt. A few books attributed to him, on magic and alchemy, survive, some poems and prayers, but very little has been translated into English. He teaches the *marifat,* knowledge of the attributes of Unity. "Those who know these things," he says, "are not themselves, but insofar as they exist at all, they exist in God." He considers the self the chief obstacle to spiritual growth, and he welcomes suffering as a means of self- discipline. "Sincerity in the search," he says, "is God's sword," and solitude also helps, for "he who is alone sees nothing but God, and if he sees only God, only God's will moves him." He associates this knowing with ecstasy, with the bewilderment of discovery, and with *hubb,* the word he uses for a love of God, which includes, he says, love for humanity. Once he was asked, "What is the end of a knower?"

"When he is as he was where he was before he was."

Attar tells another story of Dhu'l-Nun. "At nightfall, he entered a ruined building where he found a jar of gold coins and jewels covered with a board on which was inscribed the name of God. His friends divided the gold and gems, but Dhu'l-Nun said, "Give me the board. My Beloved's name is on it." All the next day he kissed the wooden board. That night he heard a voice in his dream saying, "Dhu'l-Nun! The others were satisfied with wealth, but you wanted only my name. Therefore, I have opened the gates of wisdom for you."

In Arabic script[1] the supreme name of God, Allah, looks like this:

"Ayaz' Work Clothes"(p. 120) — Ayaz, in folk tradition, was the favorite servant of Sultan Mahmud of Ghazna (971-1030). In Rumi's *Mathnawi* he appears as an example of a True Human Being: a master of surrender and a joyful slave of God. (See also the story of his crushing the king's pearl in *Delicious Laughter.*)

[1] This is early cursive script from a letter sent by the Prophet Muhammed to the ruler of al-Hasa in the seventh century. It is reproduced in Y. H. Safadi's *Islamic Calligraphy* (Boston: Shambhala, 1979).

## Afterword

One theme of this collection taken from Rumi's *Mathnawi*[1] is the nature of work, how it's a companionship rather than a competition.

I had a teacher (Bawa Muhaiyaddeen), who was definitely a one-handed basketmaker. Everything was free in Bawa's room, and he was always in deep partnership with emptiness. He sat on his bed and responded to questions. He cooked for whoever came, directing the operation from bed. He taught me how to chop onions, how to clean out a coconut and when to add those precious shreddings to the greens. He sang pure praise songs, spontaneously. He's not widely known. I'll repeat here a story he used to tell to give you the flavor.

### The Art Contest[2]

Once there was a King, who was interested in music
and dancing and drama and higher education.

He told his minister, "I want to hear good music
and see dancing and dramatic performances.
How can we arrange this?"

"May it please your Majesty,
*all* the people in this country are accomplished musicians
and actors and dancers, so that if we invite one group,
we will offend another group. We must let it be known
that there will be a competition six months from now
and that the winners will get a prize from the King."

So a great stage was built in an open area
of a thousand acres. The contest was announced,
and everyone, down to the age of six months,
started training themselves in music and acting.

The entire population stopped doing any other work!
There was hardly any food. Everyone got sickly and tired.

[1] R. A. Nicholson, *The Mathnawi of Jalaluddin Rumi*, 8 vols. (London: Luzac & Co., 1925–40). Critical edition, translation, and commentary.

[2] Bawa Muhaiyaddeen, *Divine Luminous Wisdom* (Philadelphia: Fellowship Press, 1977), pp. 77–80.

Everyone's face lost its beautiful radiance,
yet they kept on practicing for the prizes.
The day came.
The huge space was filled with artists.
There was a pavillion for the King and below it
a smaller stage which would hold
about twenty-five people, and all around that
was the entire population of the country.
Children three years old, people on the verge
of death, everyone was there.

The King asked the minister to blow the conch shell
and tell the audience to stand to one side
and the competitors on the other.

It was done, and there was no audience.
Everyone was a competitor!
The King turned to the teacher
seated beside him, "What shall I do?"
"Let them all dance and sing and act at once,
and then decide who's the best."

So they did, and the noise was horrendous.
You couldn't distinguish one voice from another.
It was like thousands of donkeys braying
and foxes howling.
"Now I see!" said the King.
"What?" asked the teacher.
"*This* is the essence
of what acting and music and dancing have become.
How can I possibly judge it!"

"Tell the artist-competitors to judge themselves.
Tell them to select the best actors and musicians
and dancers and send them to the front."

And he did, and fighting broke out, and it did not end.
The stage became a battlefield.
Eventually, no one was left alive.

The teacher said, "The corpses of these
who lost their wisdom
are the only appropriate trophies.
The vultures are the winners!"

In that same way God made the world,
and everyone came with a billion different costumes
and hypnotic illusion-projections, and the event
got so chaotic and degraded and violent
with all the competing religions and the complicated
philosophical systems and the art-status titles,
and with everyone aggressively pushing to be impressive,
and with no one there like the King
as just an eager audience,
so the prize couldn't be given.
He kept it *in Himself.*

The Kingdom of God is what there is to win,
and that's *within*. It's very rare
that someone comes and just watches with the King
and so receives the prize within
the King.

There's the disaster of everyone working in competition. If I hadn't visited Bawa's room in Philadelphia several times a year for nine years, I don't think I would have much sense of who Rumi is. He encouraged me with the translation work. "It has to be done." In fact, in the synchronicity of such things, it was some early rephrasings of Rumi that brought me to Bawa in the first place, or almost the first place. I sent some tentative attempts to a friend (Milner Ball) who was teaching at Rutgers University, Camden branch. He read them, inexplicably, to his law class. A student[3] came up afterward, asked about the poems and started writing to me, long letters, about a Sri Lankan master who was living at the time in Philadelphia. Finally, on the way to poetry readings up East, I stopped in. The cooperation is complex, and it continues.

I love it when the presence of the scribe, Husam Chelebi, appears in the *Mathnawi*. Book IV opens with, "Husam,

[3] Anyone who wants information on the Bawa Fellowship, the publications or the meetings, should contact this man, now a very focused Philadelphia lawyer, Jonathan Granoff, also known as Ahamed Muhaiyaddeen. He will be happy to help. (124 Colwyn Lane, Bala Cynwyd, PA 19004; 215-664-996, FAX 215-664-2712.)

I feel your pull again, drawing this *Mathnawi* God knows where." Rumi referred to the entire *Mathnawi* as "The Book of Husam." The poetry is a collaboration. He needs Husam closeby to allow the stories and commentary to flow. For twelve years they collected into six volumes.

Throughout, there are many passages about *working* with language:

"God has said,
*The images that come with human language*
*do not correspond to me,*
*but those who love words*
*must use them to come near.*"

In a groggy fumbling of images and sounds, language simultaneously hides and reveals the blazing inner presence. One metaphor that Rumi explores in this regard is that of words as a watery medium, something to heat up and bathe in. Stories and poems *carry messages* from the fire to your skin. We need that intermediary, he says, to keep from being burnt, and to stay clean. Word-work is warmed water, contact with the presence felt as a flowing-ness that cleans. "Enjoy this being washed with a secret we sometimes know, and then not."

Several bird poems here also involve work, the teaming up of king and falcon being a *working* twosome. Separated from the king, the falcon can't do the work he's been trained for. "With" is the key word. Rumi praises what's done in tandem. When the falcon is not *with* the king, he gets trapped and degraded. Then, something as close and practical as one's own right hand comes to assist, and a powerful new flow begins.

"You look down,
and it's lucid dreaming.
. . . You see in."

Rumi has also called the helping presence *Silence,* and the *Witness,* and *Grace.* Companionship work may be as simple as letting water move more freely in a clogged creek. One of its basic properties seems to be helplessness. A one-handed man collects withes and begins, somehow, to weave. A chick inside an egg pierces the shell and stands precariously in the open. That pecking out is poetry, the experience of where two worlds not only touch, but braid and begin something new.

Authentic work is always a friendship. Studs Terkel interviewed Nick Lindsay, a carpenter-poet, who speaks very beautifully of driving nails:

> "Every once in a while there's stuff that comes in on you. All of a sudden something falls into place. Suppose you're driving an eight-penny galvanized nail into this siding. Your whole universe is rolled onto the head of that nail. Each lick is sufficient to justify your life. You say, 'Okay, I'm not trying to get this nail out of the way so I can get onto something more important. There's nothing more important. It's right there.' And it goes—pow! It's not getting that nail in that's in your mind. It's hitting it—hitting it square, hitting it straight. Getting it now. That one lick.
>
> If you see a carpenter that's alive to his work, you'll notice that about the way he hits a nail. Although he may be working fast, each lick is like a separate person that he's hitting with his hammer. It's as though there's a separate friend of his that one moment. And when he gets out of it, here comes another one. Unique, all by itself."

> (*Working*, p. 672)

This carpenter and Rumi would agree that work is a wholehearted attention to the moment and that being so completely present is love.

Coleman Barks                                    May 2, 1991

# Rumi Books and Tapes
## Available from Maypop

*Open Secret* (Threshold, 1984) — 83 pp. A selection of odes, quatrains, and selections from the *Mathnawi*, with Introduction. Winner of a Pushcart Writers' Choice Award. $8.00.

*Unseen Rain* (Threshold, 1986) — 83 pp. One hundred and fifty short poems from Rumi's *Rubaiyat*, with Introduction. $8.00.

*We Are Three* (Maypop, 1987) — 87 pp. Odes, quatrains, and sections of the *Mathnawi*. With notes. $7.50.

*These Branching Moments* (Copper Beech, 1988) — 52 pp. Forty odes, with Introduction. $6.95.

*This Longing* (Threshold, 1988) — 107 pp. Sections from the *Mathnawi*, and Letters, with Introductions. $9.00.

*Delicious Laughter* (Maypop, 1989) — 128 pp. Rambunctious teaching stories and other more lyric sections from the *Mathnawi*, with Introduction. $7.50.

*Like This* (Maypop, 1989) — 68 pp. Forty-three odes, with Introduction. $7.50.

*Feeling the Shoulder of the Lion* (Threshold, 1991) — 103 pp. Selections from *The Mathnawi*, with introduction. $9.00.

*Open Secret* audio cassette (1987) — Various selections read by Dorothy Fadiman and Coleman Barks, with musical accompaniment. $9.95.

*Poems of Rumi*, a two-cassette package (2½ hrs). Poems read by Robert Bly and Coleman Barks, with various musical accompaniments. $15.95.

*Like This* audio cassette — Rumi poems read by Coleman Barks, with musical accompaniment by Hamza el-Din and Huzur Coughlin. $9.95.

New Dimensions Radio Interview (1986) — Coleman Barks discusses Rumi with interviewer Michael Thoms (1 hr.). $7.00.

Postage and Handling: all items: $1.50 for the first, and 50¢ for each additional item. Order from: MAYPOP BOOKS, 196 Westview Drive, Athens, GA 30606. Telephone (404) 543-2148. FAX (404) 542-2181.